THE CHRIST OF THE LOGIA

A. T. ROBERTSON
M.A., D.D., LL.D., LITT.D.

THE CHRIST OF THE LOGIA

BY

A. T. ROBERTSON

M.A., D.D., LL.D., LITT.D.

PROFESSOR OF NEW TESTAMENT INTERPRETATION,
SOUTHERN BAPTIST THEOLOGICAL SEMINARY,
LOUISVILLE, KENTUCKY.

"Art Thou the Coming One or are we to look for another?"

WIPF & STOCK · Eugene, Oregon

Wipf and Stock Publishers
199 W 8th Ave, Suite 3
Eugene, OR 97401

The Christ of the Logia
By Robertson, A. T.
ISBN 13: 978-1-62032-674-9
Publication date 12/15/2012
Previously published by George H. Doran, 1924

TO

THE MEMORY OF

MY SISTER MAUD

WHOSE BRIGHT SPIRIT

HAS CHEERED ME ALL THE WAY

PREFACE

The essays in the present book deal with the greatest question of all the ages, that put by Jesus to the Pharisees and Sadducees at the close of the great temple debate: "What think ye of the Christ?" (Matt. 22:42). That question is still the touchstone of all high thinking and right living. Old Simeon had said of the Babe: "Behold, this *child* is set for the falling and the rising of many in Israel" (Luke 2: 34). And Jesus boldly denounced the conspirators at the end who had rejected Him: "And he that falleth on this stone shall be broken to pieces: but on whomsoever it shall fall, it will scatter him as dust" (Matt. 21:44). The world has tried to do without Jesus, but it has failed. Men have tried hypocrisy, but Jesus at last uncovers the wolf beneath the sheepskin. They have denounced Him as a dreamer and as in the way of the progress of the superman, but the very wrath of man has turned to praise at last. The law of the jungle in war and rapine and selfishness have driven man back to the foot of the Cross. The law of love is the law of life. The whole world lay in the grip of the evil one in John's day (1 John 5:19). The only deliverer now as then is Jesus. Men have tried to laugh sin away, but the grim reality mocks their laughter. Scholarship has dealt relentlessly with the sources of our knowledge of Jesus according to the severest tests of modern science. Some thought that the new knowledge had explained Jesus away as a myth of the morning or a legend of the night. But Jesus remains after all is done. He stands forth in clearer light than ever before. He stands on the heights of purity and of pity and calls to a lost and ruined world to follow him as of old. In these essays the facts of modern research are faced with candor. The weapons that scholarship once used against Christ are turned against His foes. The Light of the world is still Jesus of Nazareth. The picture is turned now this way, now that. But each facet shows the Christ of faith and of hope to be the Jesus of history and of life. The Greeks still come and say: "Sir, we would see Jesus." May we be able to show Him to the seekers after Truth. The lesson of real scholarship is humility and reverence. The oldest document about Christ known to modern scholarship, the so-called Logia of Jesus, pictures the same Jesus seen in the rest of the New Testament. Good will come out of the new interest in the Virgin Birth, the Resurrection, and the actual Deity of Jesus Christ. Men will be brought back to a fresh and prolonged study of the records of Christ in the New Testament and in human history. The more men know of Christ the more worship they will give Him.

Louisville, Ky. A. T. Robertson.

ACKNOWLEDGMENT

The following journals have consented to the use of the chapters that first appeared in their columns: *The Contemporary Review,* the *Christian Worker's Magazine,* the *Christian Index, The Methodist Review* (Nashville), *The Homiletic Review, The Expositor* (London), *The Constructive Quarterly, The Biblical World* and *The Biblical Review.*

CONTENTS

THE CHRIST OF THE LOGIA

THE CHRIST OF THE LOGIA

Chapter I

THE CHRIST OF THE LOGIA

1. *The Quest for Christ*

The Greeks, who said to Philip at the last passover in the ministry of our Lord, "Sir, we would see Jesus" (John xii, 21), reflect the present intellectual temper of men. It has not always been easy to find Christ. Philip and Andrew were greatly puzzled by the courteous request of the Greeks. John the Baptist said to the committee of the Sanhedrin: "There standeth one among you, whom ye know not" (John i, 26). It is quite certain that not all those who try to point out Jesus Christ to men can do so. There is much of truth in Schweitzer's *The Quest of the Historical Jesus* (Tr., 1910). The scholars have zigzagged through the centuries and have not followed the same path or reached the same goal. Schweitzer, himself a German critic, turns upon his fellow German critics who are not eschatologists, with the fierce charge: "As formerly in

Renan the romantic spirit created the personality of Jesus in its own image so at the present day the Germanic spirit is making a Jesus after its own likeness" (*ibid.*, p. 307). Bluntly he says: "The liberal Jesus has given place to the Germanic Jesus." The dust of criticism is more or less necessary, like that in the mill, but it is only justified if one gets good flour from the grist. Schweitzer sees Jesus only in a mist and is afraid that the fog will not lift. "The names in which men expressed their recognition of Him as such, Messiah, Son of Man, Son of God, have become for us historical parables. We can find no designation which expresses what He is for us" (*ibid.*, p. 401). So he leaves Jesus "an ineffable mystery."

But criticism promised to give us the historical Jesus in distinction from the theological Christ of Paul and John. Paul was brushed aside by certain critics in the "Jesus or Paul" controversy. John's Gospel was denied historical value because of its philosophical interpretation in favor of the objective Jesus of the Synoptic Gospels. In the Synoptics we should find the real Jesus of fact, set free from the later perversions of Paul and the apotheosis of the Fourth Gospel which could not be considered Johannine in any historical sense.

But Synoptic criticism will not allow us to take the picture of Jesus drawn in these Gospels as it stands. Luke is a disciple of Paul and naturally reflects the Pauline Christology. Matthew's Gospel is probably the Logia rewritten by Matthew or by someone else to prove the thesis that Jesus of Nazareth is the Jewish Messiah. But at bottom the Christ of Matthew and Luke does not differ in essential outline from the Christ of John and Paul. The shading differs, but we have the same God-man in all four pictures. Matthew and Luke give further offense to many critics by the story of the Virgin Birth. The Johannine and the Pauline Christ is the object of worship and is credited with essential deity. The germs at least of this conception are manifest in Matthew and Luke. Away, then, with Paul who made Christ out of Jesus and who cares nothing for the historical Jesus. Away with John who actually applies the word God to Christ. So the argument ran.

Now Christian scholars cannot refuse to face any facts, whatever theories they hold. Criticism is merciless in dealing with theories, however sacred. One has no right to complain of rigid scientific research into the facts. This is what all men should desire. Only one must be sure of the facts. It matters not what the real attitude of a critic may be toward Jesus. One must patiently examine all the facts that are presented in order to be sure that they are facts.

The one certain result of Synoptic criticism is that both Matthew and Luke made use of Mark and a non-Markan document called Q or the

Logia of Jesus. They probably used various other sources also. Luke certainly did, for he speaks of "many" (Luke i, 1-4). The others we do not possess, but Mark is with us and Q is agreed to be at least the non-Markan material that appears in both Matthew and Luke. Thus, then, we have two pictures of Jesus that antedate our present Matthew and Luke. Our Greek Matthew may or may not be the work of the man who wrote Q (the Logia of Papias probably). It was inevitable that a close examination should be made of the picture of Jesus in Mark and in Q.

2. *The Priority of Q*

Wellhausen (*Einleitung in die drei ersten Evangelien,* pp. 73-89) argues strongly in favor of the priority of Mark to Q. But he has not been followed by the consensus of modern opinion. Harnack (*The Sayings of Jesus,* tr., p. 194) is positive that Q precedes Mark. Indeed, Streeter (*Oxford Studies in the Synoptic Problem,* 1911, pp. 165-183) contends that Mark shows knowledge and use of Q. The examples are not numerous, but reasonably clear. "The cumulative effect of these instances is irresistible, and must establish beyond a reasonable doubt that Mark was familiar with Q." How long before Mark was Q in existence? Streeter (*ibid.,* p. 219) says: "If our characterization of Q above is correct, it was probably written twenty years before Mark, and might well have reached Rome before him." We are not here concerned with the actual date of Mark, though there are those who put it as early as 50 A.D. If Luke wrote his Gospel before Acts and wrote Acts while he was in Rome during Paul's first imprisonment, Mark cannot come later than 60 A.D., probably much earlier. If Q is twenty years earlier than Mark, it is entirely possible that Ramsay (*The Expositor,* May, 1907) and Salmon (*The Human Element in the Gospels,* p. 274) are correct in thinking that Q was written during the lifetime of Jesus, and for this reason does not include the Passion Week. But that inferential date is not necessary.

3. From Mark to Q

But if Mark gives us Peter's interpretation of Jesus, surely we can feel secure in the Markan picture of Christ. In Mark we have the earliest narrative of the life of Jesus, or, at least, of certain parts of His ministry. Here in Mark there is little theology and more objective history. But Mark has fared no better than Matthew, Luke, Paul, and John. Pfleiderer, for instance, feels that the appeal from Paul to the Synoptics has not gotten rid of Paul. "Little as it can be denied that the apologetic motives of the general Gospel tradition and Pauline views of faith in particular are dominant, yet a comparison with the other Gospels reveals that Mark represents an earlier stage of apologetic authorship, and hence a comparatively clearer and more naïve presentation of tradition" (*Christian Origins*, tr., p. 217). Pfleiderer refuses to believe that Mark has correctly reported Peter's interpretation of Jesus. Rather he accuses Mark of reading Paul into Peter's tradition: "The pupil of Paul is most evident in the speeches, which the Evangelist did not find in his source-book or in the Palestinian tradition, but created independently and for the first time fitted into the traditional material as the leading religious motives for the judgment of the history of Jesus" (*ibid.*, p. 220). We are not here concerned with answering Pfleiderer. The point is to show that the appeal from Paul to Mark, once heralded as the simple historical narrator of the earthly life of Jesus, has not brought satisfaction to the critics of Paul's theological vagaries. In a word, Pfleiderer holds that Mark's Gospel "unites the Jesus of the Palestinian tradition, the energetic hero of a Jewish reform movement, with the Christ of the Pauline theology" (*ibid.*, p. 222). Already, then, according to Pfleiderer, in Mark Jesus has become Christ. Christianity has already passed through the "Jesus or Christ" controversy, so ably discussed in the *Hibbert Journal* during 1909.

If, then, we wish to know the story of Jesus in its simplest pre-Pauline, pre-theological form, we must go behind Mark. We have only Q left to which to go. If Q fails us, we are poor indeed, in our knowledge of the historical Jesus, according to this critical theory. Bacon is sure that "Mark is devoutly Pauline" (*Hibbert Journal Supplement*, 1909, p. 214), but thinks that he can pick out in Mark "the Petrine tradition of Jesus' earthly career" whch "reduces itself upon critical scrutiny to this simple residuum" as "the figure of the prophet whom God according to promise had raised up among his brethren, and sent him to bless them in turning away every one of them from their iniquities," as compared with Mark's "transcendental thaumaturgist" (*ibid.*, pp. 215*f.*). Even in Mark, under Pauline influence, Bacon thinks that "a long step has been taken on the road to apotheosis." What Bacon calls for is "the figure of Jesus presented by the primitive Matthew" (Q), "the ideal scribe of the kingdom of heaven, a prophet like unto Moses" (*ibid.*, p. 216), for "Mark is a thoroughly Pauline Gospel" (p. 213). Bacon asks this question: "What relative value appears to be attached to the Pauline conception of the gospel *sub specie æternitatis*, and the pre-Pauline, as we go backward from Mark to Q?" (pp. 212*f.*). Both Peter and Paul presented "Jesus as Lord," and so "Peter's gospel was indeed identical with Paul's."

It is plain, therefore, that criticism must turn to Q to see what sort of a picture of Jesus is given there. Bacon rejoices that "that Pauline, Greek interpretation of 'the gospel' is coming to an end" (p. 219). Has it come to an end? No one can complain that "the keen scalpel of historical criticism has been applied to the evangelic tradition" (*ibid*). One could not wish it otherwise. There is nothing to conceal about Jesus. The full truth and only the truth is what all wish to know. But criticism itself must be criticised. "How much remains of 'the Christ of religion' when we reach that earliest element of Synoptic tradition, Q, the one source generally acknowledged by both the most ancient and the most modern inquiry to be truly apostolic in authorship and historical in intuition?" (*ibid.*, p. 216). We must then look squarely at Q if we wish to follow the path of historical criticism in the search for the earliest picture of Jesus. Bacon takes Q to be the same as Papias' Logia of Jesus, which he attributes to the Apostle Matthew. He thinks that Papias is correct. The Johannine authorship of the Fourth Gospel is denied by many and discredited by others as too theological even if apostolic. Luke's Gospel is not apostolic at all, and is written by a Greek. Mark's Gospel is apostolic only in so far as it correctly reports Peter's sermons about Jesus and is free from "Pauline" influence. We have left only Q as the safe and sure foundation for our picture of the original "Jesus of History." To Q, then, let us go.

4. The Limits of Q

It is quite important, before we proceed, to learn, if we can, what sort of a document Q was. In a rough-and-ready sort of way, Harnack confines his study of Q to "the relatively original text of the sections which are exclusively common to St. Matthew and St. Luke." (*The Sayings of Jesus,* tr., p. xiv.) But it must be borne in mind that our Q is a torso, for we do not know how extensive a document it really was and we are not justified in drawing conclusions about what is not in the quotations made by Matthew and Luke. Harnack, for instance, puts this sentence in italics (*The Sayings of Jesus,* p. 248): "The influence of 'Paulinism' which is so strong in St. Mark is entirely wanting, and accordingly the main theme of St. Mark—that Jesus, His death and resurrection, form the content of His own gospel—is not to be found in Q." The argument from silence is always precarious and is not to be made thus prominent. No doubt, Q is wholly free from Paulinism, for its early date precludes that result. But how does Harnack know that Q, the original document, had nothing about the death and resurrection of Jesus? Bacon sees the peril of this path and says: "We need not go to the full length of Harnack's astounding conclusion that this most primitive of all attempts to embody the 'Way' of Christian faith *had no mention whatever of passion or resurrection*" (*Hibbert*

Journal Supplement, p. 216). Streeter discusses "the original Extent of Q" in very able fashion in the *Oxford Studies in the Synoptic Problem* (pp. 185-208). He asks what we should do to restore Mark if Mark had been lost and Q preserved. If we only credited to Mark what *both* Matthew and Luke use, we should have only two-thirds of our Mark. "We infer therefore that the passages which we can *identify as Q* by the fact that *both* Matthew and Luke reproduce them *may* possibly only represent about two-thirds of the original total matter in Q" (p. 185). That seems a perfectly fair statement of the problem. Hence it is possible, even probable, that some of the non-Markan matter peculiar either to Matthew or Luke in reality comes from Q. "The attempt to ascertain which of the passages which now appear as 'peculiar' to Matthew or Luke were derived from Q is naturally one of great interest, but it cannot be too often emphasized that it is at best careful guessing" (Streeter, *ibid.*, p. 186). Streeter suggests the possibility that Luke derived from Q "the bulk of the two blocks ix. 51-xv. 10 and xvii. i-xviii. 8" (*ibid.*, p. 206). Who can say, then, that Q did not contain anything concerning the death and resurrection of Jesus? Mark's account we have and that of Matthew and Luke. If Q extended thus far, Matthew and Luke may have preferred Mark's orderly narrative or may have employed both accounts. In reports of the trial, death and resurrection of Jesus neither

Matthew nor Luke always follows Mark nor do they always give the same items or in the same way. It is quite possible that Q was used by them throughout the great narrative of the Passion and Resurrection of Our Lord.

Another word of caution is given by W. C. Allen, in his paper on "The Book of Sayings used by the Editor of the First Gospel" (*Oxford Studies in the Synoptic Problem*, pp. 235-287). He insists that the "colourless symbol Q (=Quelle)" is preferable to the Logia of Papias because the term Logia implies in many minds that Q contained only discourses. This is not the necessary or the probable idea of Papias, but Q does have this advantage over Logia. But Harnack himself, who urges the term Q, is not willing to let the report of the Baptist's preaching and the temptation of Jesus (clearly Q as given only by Matthew and Luke) to belong to Q without a question mark. He says: "If we consider Q apart from its introduction (sections 1 and 2), we see at once that we are dealing with a document of the highest antiquity—there is here no need of proof; but even if we take into our view Q together with the introduction, there is little difference in the final verdict" (*Sayings of Jesus*, p. 246). Harnack proceeds to argue that the idea that Jesus was endowed with the Messiahship at the baptism is incapable of proof or disproof. So Harnack has to brush aside the first two sections of his Q as too theological, just like Mark and the rest. One is bound to bring against Harnack the charge of theological prepossession against the deity of Jesus. On page 244 he admits that, according to Q, "Jesus was the Messiah, consecrated as Son of God at the Baptism." But he adds in italics: "If, however, we think away the introduction, the resultant picture is essentially different," though he elsewhere explained that it made little difference. Critical processes are here thrown aside by Harnack in the interest of his theological prejudice. He can only find his picture of the original Christ by "thinking away" the introduction in Q.

5. *The Atmosphere of Q*

Bacon contends that while "the tests of historical criticism have been applied to the evangelic tradition of the Galilean Apostles," "the gospel of Paul calls for quite another form of criticism. After the historian and interpreter have done their work, the psychologist and philosopher must have their say" (*Hibbert Journal Supplement*, p. 221). But we have just seen that Harnack will not allow that Q is purely objective and historical, though he places Q above Mark in historical value (*Sayings of Jesus*, p. 226). "The Galilean horizon, within which Q seems to move more exclusively than St. Mark, must be simply accepted as an historical fact" (*ibid.*, p. 227). And yet Wellhausen makes Q everywhere secondary to Mark in historical importance. Jülicher is of the opinion that Q grew by degrees, and was even later than Mark in its last edition. So we do not seem to come to any solid agreement after all about Q. Wellhausen finds Q of secondary worth because of its definite Christology and ecclesiasticism. But Harnack makes "the observation that Q has no interest in Christological apologetics such as would explain the choice of the arrangement, and the coloring of the discourses and sayings it contains. In this Q shows itself absolutely different from St. Mark, St. Matthew, and St. John. St. Luke here stands nearest to Q." One would think that Harnack finds Q wholly historical and reliable in its picture of Jesus. But he makes important reservations concerning the stories of the Baptist's preaching and Christ's temptation (Sections 1 and 2), Section 25 about the Son's knowledge of the Father, and the announcement of the Second Coming (*Sayings of Jesus*, pp. 234*f*.). With this concession Harnack agrees that, although Q was not compiled in the interests of Christological apologetics, it is nevertheless rich in discourses and sayings in which special prominence is given and special attention is drawn to the personality of Jesus (*ibid.*, p. 235). But why eliminate Sections 1, 2, and 25? It is time, then, to see what Q does say about Jesus.

6. *Points About the Personality of Jesus*

Bacon says that in Q "the Jesus of history appears in the simple light of a champion of the 'unchurched' Israelite protesting against the usurped authority of the scribes" (*Hibbert Journal Supplement,* p. 219). That is true. But is that all that is true? Von Soden thinks that by means of our Gospel of Matthew (Q and Mark) "Peter triumphs over Paul and the historical Jesus over the metaphysical Christ" (*The History of Early Christian Literature,* tr., p. 200). But is not the Christ of Mark, Matthew, Luke, John, Paul in Q? We have seen that Harnack is afraid that this is true, though he tries hard to "think away" the "Christ" from Q. He draws a distinction between the "compiler" of Q and the "source," the original Q, used by the compiler. But even so, note this from Harnack: "The 'Christology' of the source, *as the compiler understood it,* presents a perfectly simple and consistent picture. The compiler of Q could not imagine otherwise than that Jesus was the Messiah, consecrated as Son of God at the Baptism" (*Sayings of Jesus,* pp. 243*f.*). But Harnack proceeds to discount every passage in Q that gives the high estimate of Jesus found in the later writings, though he admits that the original Q had these sayings. One is bound to say that as a matter of scientific and historical interpretation, one is not here concerned with

Harnack's view of Christ. We have that in his *What is Christianity?* What we desire is to see the Christ of Q, and that Harnack whittles down to a "reduced" Jesus in his discussion of "The Personality of Our Lord" in Q. What did Jesus claim about himself in Q? Do we find the same terms applied to him here as in the later documents? Is he regarded as the Son of God, the Son of Man, the Messiah? If we agree as to what Q contained, then we must let Q speak whether we agree with its Christology or no. It is unscientific and mere apologetic criticism to twist Q to modern notions of Jesus.

Let us begin with "the Son of God" in Harnack's Q. Twice in Section 2 (the temptation) the devil calls Jesus "Son of God" in a conditional clause of the first class that assumes the reality of the condition (εἰ υἱὸς εἶ τοῦ θεοῦ). It matters little that this testimony is reported as from the devil. The point is that it is recorded in Q. All three temptations turn on this issue of the Sonship of Jesus. The devil puts Jesus' consciousness of his peculiar Sonship to the test. Besides, this language in the mouth of the devil refers beyond a doubt to the voice of the Father at the Baptism which appears in the Markan tradition. Harnack (*Sayings of Jesus,* p. 235) admits that "Q probably proceeded to narrate the baptism of Our Lord, together with the descent of the Spirit and the voice from heaven, by which he was marked off as the Son of God (the Messiah) in the sense of Ps. ii. 7." But in the account of the temptation in Q Jesus does not deny that he is the Son of God. He assumes that he is so securely that as not to require to prove it. He and the Father understand one another. This Messianic consciousness meets us at the very beginning of the ministry of Jesus as presented in Q, and refutes at once the idea that Jesus only later came to perceive that he was the Son of God or the Messiah.

But there is also the famous "Johannine" passage in Q (Harnack's Section 25: Matt. xi. 25-7; Luke x. 21*f.*), where Jesus uses "the Father" and "the Son" in precisely the manner of John's Gospel. This absolute use of "the Father" and "the Son" appears also in Mark xiii. 32. Harnack admits the genuineness of this passage, but says (*Sayings of Jesus,* p. 219): "The conclusion: 'No man hath knowledge of the Father except the Son, and he to whomsoever the Son willeth to reveal Him,' says nothing about an 'eternal' relationship between the Father and the Son, but simply expresses an historical fact." Here Harnack makes an effort to avoid the implication of the deity of the Son. The logion is a universal statement, and is as timeless as the Greek knows how to make it. It is wholly gratuitous to say that Jesus meant this claim to cover only His life here on earth. The consciousness behind this sentence is not that of a mere man. Harnack even says that this peculiar relationship of Jesus as the Son to the Father "does not lie beyond the line" of the passage about a greater than Jonah and Solomon. *Per contra,* Allen (*International Critical Commentary on Matthew,* pp. 306*f.*) argues that the presence of the antithesis "the Father, the Son" in Matthew xi. 27 (as in Mark xiii. 32) shows that "the combination 'the Son, the Father,' was also familiar to the source from which he was drawing (The Matthæan Logia). This antithesis 'the Father—the Son' is, above all, characteristic of the Fourth Gospel." But it is present in Q, and offers the historic background for the Trinitarian conception in our earliest Christian document. On page 241 Harnack says of Section 25 (the passage about the relations of the Father and the Son) and Section 20: "It forms the climax of Our Lord's self-revelation, and yet it does not assert more than that He had been permitted to bring to the simple ones the knowledge of God." This is a rather easy way to empty language of its obvious meaning. The fact that Jesus claims to be the Son of God and is so called in Q is beyond dispute, however one may explain the language.

What about the Son of Man in Q? Harnack's Q has "the Son of Man" in Sections 15, 17, 30, 34 *a, b,* 37, 56. Three of these are eschatological, but the other four are not. Harnack can only say: "We must acknowledge that in Q the phrase has become simply a term which our Lord ordinarily used when speaking of Himself." (*Sayings of Jesus*, p. 238). "There can scarcely be any doubt as to the sense of the expression in Q." "In Q the term can mean nothing else than the Messiah." It is worth while to quote these passages: "The Son of Man hath not where to lay His head," "The Son of Man will acknowledge those who confess Him," "A word said against the Son of Man will be forgiven," "The Son of Man came eating and drinking," "As Jonah was to the Ninevites, so is the Son of Man become a sign to this generation," "As the days of Noah, so will be the coming of the Son of Man." Clearly, then, Q knows Jesus as "the Son of God" and "the Son of Man."

Is Jesus "the Messiah" in Q? We have seen that Harnack so interprets "the Son of Man." But what about "the Christ" (ὁ Χριστός)? The term occurs once only in Section 14. "John, hearing in prison the works of the Christ," sent to ask of Jesus: "Art thou the Coming One or are we to look for another?" Harnack (*Sayings of Jesus*, p. 239) thinks that this is the most important passage in Q concerning the personality of our Lord, because here Jesus appeals to His works in proof of His Messiahship. But there is no particle of doubt that in the background of Q there is always the implication on the part of Jesus: "I am the Messiah." The very last passage in Harnack's Q has this logion: "Ye, that follow me, shall sit upon twelve thrones judging the twelve tribes of Israel." Harnack adds: "This saying affords us to very strongest imaginable testimony that Q is dominated by the belief in the Messiahship; the fact of the Messiahship is proved in the introduction; it is presupposed as self-evident from the beginning to the end of the work, and in the eschatological discourses it is revealed by Jesus Himself" (*Sayings of Jesus*, p. 243). Harnack considers it "unthinkable" (p. 246) that Jesus considered Himself a "present Messiah." He holds that in Q it is only in the eschatological passages that "the Messiah is clearly expressed under the form of the Parousia" (p. 245). So sure is Harnack that Jesus is not the present Messiah that he translates Peter's confession, "Thou art the Messiah" by "Thou wilt be He!" But, in seeking to find out what Q teaches concerning the Messiahship of Jesus it is best not to dogmatize too much. The fact of the Messiahship of Jesus in Q is beyond dispute. Four of the seven passages that have "the Son of Man" are ethical, not eschatological, sayings. It is at least open to question whether Jesus in the eschatological passages in Q is not thinking of the Second Coming rather than the first. The Parousia of the "Son of Man" (Section 56) seems to be the same event as the unexpected hour for which the disciples were to be ready (Section 37).

In Section 12 (the close of the Sermon on the Mount) Jesus speaks of those who call him "Lord,

Lord" (κύριε, κύριε) where the language seems more than mere address. The word in the Septuagint is common for God. In the papyri and inscriptions it is frequent for the Roman Emperor, who is regarded as divine. The use here in Q by Jesus reminds one of Paul's language in First Corinthians xii. 1-3, where "Lord" is not applied lightly to Jesus.

But these terms of Messianic dignity (the Son of God, the Son of Man, the Christ, Lord) do not stand alone in Q. The consciousness of Jesus throughout Q is of a piece with these epithets. John the Baptist (Section 1) says: "He that cometh after me is mightier than I, whose shoes I am not worthy to bear." The tone of Jesus in the Sermon on the Mount (Section 6) is that of superiority to the current teaching of the rabbis and to the Old Testament, which he proceeds to complete and carry further. Christ's "But I say unto you" was language of arrogance to many, unless he was what he claimed to be. Jesus concludes the Sermon on the Mount (Section 12) by making His words the rock on which the house must be built that will stand the wind and the floods. It is hard to imagine a higher claim. And the centuries have justified this claim of Jesus as we find it in Q. The hope of the world to-day is that it may at last get itself planted on the teaching of Jesus. The world war has made this point plain. In Section 13 Jesus commends the centurion's faith in him in contrast to the scepticism of the Jews: "Not even in Israel have I found so great faith." Ho makes himself the *crux* of the relation of men to God. In the reply of the Baptist (Section 14) Jesus claims to be the Messiah as proven by his works, and rebukes the momentary doubt of the Baptist: "And blessed is he that does not find occasion of stumbling in me." Here, again, Jesus is conscious of his Messiahship, and holds faith in himself the supreme test of a man's destiny. In fact, Jesus puts following himself above all other duties, even that of remaining till one's father dies and is buried (Section 17). "Follow me," Jesus demanded, "and let the dead bury their own dead." Jesus claims that "all things were delivered unto me by the Father" (Section 5). Taken in the absolute sense, this language implies deity. It comes in the famous Johannine passage about "the Father" and "the Son." But, taken in a limited sense, it is still a very high claim, and carries a meaning of conscious superiority. Jesus is constantly making his own person and mission the test. "He that is not with me is against me" (Section 29). He is greater than Jonah and greater than Solomon (Section 30). Confession of Jesus is made the test for admission to the Father's presence. "Everyone who confesses me before men, him will the Son of Man confess before the angels of God; but whoever denies Me before men, him will I deny before the angels of God" (Sections 34a). This is not the language of an ordinary prophet or teacher. Indeed Jesus speaks of Himself as belonging to the same plane as the Holy Spirit (compare "the Father" and "the Son"). "And whoever speaks a word against the Son of Man, it shall be forgiven him; but whoever speaks against the Holy Spirit, it shall not be forgiven him" (Section 34b). One cannot well think of a mere man using language like this, even though in this matter he places himself below the Holy Spirit. Once more take this passage (Section 38): "Do you think that I came to bring peace upon the earth? I came not to bring peace, but a sword. For I came to set a man against his father and a daughter against her mother and a bride against her husband." Here is a cosmic consciousness of world relations that is timeless and universal and imperative.

Men have to face the problem of Jesus as He himself sees it in Q. The impending doom of Jerusalem is due to the rejection of Jesus. They will not see him again till they say: "Blessed is he that cometh in the name of the Lord" (Section 43). At least it must be admitted that Jerusalem was destroyed after Q was written. So, then, Jesus did foretell this dire event and made it turn on the attitude of Jerusalem to himself. And it must be admitted also that not yet have the Jews been restored to Jerusalem. At last Christians have won it from the Turks. And what shall one say of a saying like this: "He that loveth father or mother more than me is not worthy of me;

and he that loveth son or daughter more than me is not worthy of me" (Section 45)? Only one who holds a supreme place can properly use language like that. So Jesus adds: "He that does not take up his cross and follow me is not worthy of me" (Section 46). In Q, as truly as in the Fourth Gospel, Jesus himself is the issue set before men. One's attitude toward Jesus is the decisive factor in human destiny. There is no dispute concerning the high claim made by Jesus in the eschatological passages like Sections 56 and 59. That will be a world event, sudden, cataclysmic, divisive in result. Harnack says plainly that "Q's aims are not those of apologetic Christology" (*Sayings of Jesus*, p. 241).

It is now clear that one has in Q the same essential picture of Jesus as the Christ that we find in the other Gospels and in Paul's Epistles. Indeed, if the presupposition that Jesus is the Christ is ground for suspicion, "one must draw the pen through the whole content of the Gospels" (Harnack, *ibid.*, p. 241). The facts in Q are open and simple and beyond reasonable dispute. One need take no position as to the chronology of the Sayings or their relative order. The order of Harnack has been followed here. But the effect is cumulative and tremendous. It is not necessary to depreciate Mark as Harnack does (*ibid.*, p. 250) as "an apologetic which grasps at all within its reach, to which everything is welcome and right." That is, I think, an unfair characterization of the Gospel of Mark. But Q is a sufficient reply to those who, like Schweitzer, make the historical Jesus a mere mistaken eschatological dreamer who was carried away by the Jewish apocalyptic teaching. "Above all, the tendency to exaggerate the apocalyptic and eschatological element in our Lord's Message, and to subordinate to this the purely religious and ethical elements, will ever find its refutation in Q" (Harnack, *ibid.*, pp. 250*f.*). Harnack is also right in saying: "The portrait of Jesus as given in the Sayings of Q has remained in the foreground" (p. 250). Harnack means as opposed to that of Mark. But that is a matter of interpretation.

Harnack approaches the study of Q with a prejudice against the deity of Jesus, and cannot resist the temptation to whittle away the sayings that show this doctrine. One may retort that the present discussion reveals a clear prejudice in favor of the deity of Jesus. Be it so. The facts are all in Q and are open to all. The facts are far more important than any man's interpretation of them. It is plain enough that a critical prejudice against the theological Christ has animated the long search for the historical Jesus. This spirit has not vitiated the scientific method or the historical results. That has all been to the good whatever theory one holds about Jesus as the Christ, the Son of God.

It is here contended as proven that the search for the historical Jesus, laudable as it is, has not gotten rid of the theological Christ. In Q Jesus is the Christ, the Son of God, the Son of Man. One may explain it as one will, but the fact remains. Harnack admits that in Q there is no evidence that there was a time when Jesus did not regard himself as the Messiah. "Q, however, gives some help in that we learn from this source how completely and quickly the consciousness, that there was once a time when our Lord did not so name Himself, had vanished from tradition" (*Sayings of Jesus,* p. 239). We may let that pass. But Q, like the Gospels, shows that the disciples were puzzled over the enigmatic sayings of Jesus, though it does not so plainly bring out the dulness of the apostles concerning the person of Jesus as is shown in Mark (doubtless from Peter himself).

We come back, therefore, in our earliest document about Jesus to the same high estimate of our Lord that we find in the latest portrait. The lines are simpler and the shading is lighter, but the essential features of the God-Man are in Q. The controversy concerning the Person of Christ is not ended by Q. The same prejudices that animated the minds of men before the discovery of Q as the result of Synoptic criticism remain. Those who refuse to credit Jesus with deity in spite of John, Paul, Luke, Matthew and Mark, will refuse to do so in spite of the fact that Q pictures Jesus as the Son of God. Those who have found Jesus to be Lord and Saviour will rejoice that in Q

He is Jesus Christ, the same yesterday, to-day, and for ever. The wonder remains how it came to pass that in Q, though the disciples were mystified by the Master, the consciousness of Jesus as Lord of life runs through all that Jesus said and did. It is plain enough if he was, in fact, the Son of God. It is certain that in Q we have the earliest picture of Jesus that has been preserved for us. One is not able to say that Luke may not have had a still earlier one among his "many." But, if Q is in reality the primitive Matthew, it is genuinely apostolic. Whether written by Matthew as notes during the ministry of Jesus or no, it at any rate preserves Matthew's report of the teachings of Jesus, and it was written very early. It is possible thus to get behind our Four Gospels. Von Soden tries to reproduce also the Petrine picture of Jesus out of Mark's Gospel. Certainly it is there, but one cannot always feel sure when Peter is Mark's source. But one will be in strict accord with modern knowledge, if one begins with Q, then takes in succession Mark, Matthew, Luke, Paul, John as interpreters of Jesus Christ. There are other pictures of Christ in the New Testament, those of James, Peter, the author of Hebrews, which can be fitted into the whole New Testament portrait, as C. Anderson Scott has done in his *Dominus Noster*. It is manifest that the impression made by Jesus during His ministry was all that the Gospels represent it to be. The heart of it all is in Q. Jesus drew men to Him or drove men away from Him while on earth in the flesh. He is still set, as Simeon said, for the falling and the rising of many. He still charms or chills those who come near Him. But no one can be indifferent to the Fact of Christ, the great Person of history. There were never so many as now who agree with Charles Lamb that in the presence of Jesus we must all bow, and, like Thomas, say: "My Lord and my God."

Chapter II

THE DEITY OF CHRIST IN THE GOSPEL OF MARK

Some scholars have misunderstood Mark in their eagerness to discredit John. They have pitted the objective Mark against the subjective John for the purpose of overthrowing the plain and unacceptable statements of the deity of Jesus in John's Gospel. That is the thesis in John's Gospel, as I sought to show in my little book, *The Divinity of Christ in the Gospel of John.* But some have been too hasty in their conclusions about Mark. The alternative is usually between John's portrait of Christ and that in the Synoptic Gospels, but at bottom that means Mark's picture of Christ which he obtained from Peter. "On this question we are driven unavoidably to the alternative; either Synoptics, or John. Either the former are right in their complete silence regarding preëxistence and incarnation, and their subordination of the doctrine of Jesus' person in presenting His work and teaching as concerned with the kingdom of God, with repentance and a filial disposition and life, as the requirement made by the common Father for that inheritance; or else John is right in making Jesus' work and message supremely a manifestation of His own glory as the incarnate Logos, effecting an atonement for the world which has otherwise no access to God. Both views cannot be true, and to a very large extent it is the science of literary criticism which must decide between them." (Bacon, *The Fourth Gospel in Restarch and Debate,* 1910, page 3).

Here Professor B. W. Bacon, of Yale University, succinctly puts the modern attack on John's Gospel behind the battery of the Synoptic Gospels. On page 13 he states it thus: "And the heart of the problem is the Gospel attributed to John, with its reversal of the synoptic conception. Both conceptions cannot represent the apostolic story. Harmonization overreaches itself when it attempts to bridge this chasm." Scott discredits John's Gospel thus: "When he discards any important element in the synoptic record, his reason invariably is that it will not blend with his own theological view" (*The Fourth Gospel: Its Purpose and Theology,* 1906, page 44). One would suppose from this line of criticism that in the Synoptic Gospels all difficulties vanish and we have smooth sailing.

Critics Contradicting Themselves

But, alas for the critics! Pfleiderer has no more patience with Mark's picture of Christ than Bacon and Scott have with John's. Pfleiderer says: "Little as it can be denied, that the apologetic motives of the general Gospel tradition and Pauline views of faith in particular are dominant, yet a comparison with the other Gospels reveals that Mark represents an earlier stage of apologetic authorship and hence a comparatively clearer and more naïve presentation of tradition'' (*Christian Origins,* tr. 1906, page 217). He admits (page 219) that ''this oldest evangelist furnishes the truest impression which Jesus made on His environment,'' but insists ''that even the oldest Gospel writer is guided by a decided apologetic purpose in the selection and manipulation of his material.'' Mark thus tries to prove Jesus of Nazareth ''to be the Christ and the Son of God by wonders and signs of every kind.'' So then even Mark is guilty of aiming to prove the deity of Jesus, according to Pfleiderer!

One is bound to admit that Pfleiderer has on this point properly interpreted Mark's Gospel. In *The Expositor* (London) for December, 1917, Rev. W. R. Whately has an article on ''Christ as the Object of Faith in the Synoptic Gospels,'' in which he shows beyond a doubt that this is true. ''The synoptic evidence in fact is really more cogent than that derived from the fourth Gospel.'' ''The Christology of the sayings and discourses recorded by the synoptists is implicit rather than explicit, and has often escaped the notice even of careful and scholarly readers.'' He goes on to show that in the synoptists Jesus claims to be the Judge of the world, demands the absolute allegiance of all men, possesses a unique knowledge of God, is the moral law giver, is King in the kingdom of the elect like Jehovah in the Old Testament, possesses miraculous powers, and has power to forgive sins like God. All this is true and more.

Indeed, so clear is it that in our canonical Mark, based on Peter's discourses, we have the same person, both divine and human, as in Paul's Epistles and John's Gospel, that efforts are made to get back of our present Mark. Wendling does it by the Ur-Marcus theory that there were three "Marks" (M^1, M^2, M^3). John Mark may have written M^1, and M^3 is our Mark. Bacon (*The Beginnings of the Gospel Story,* 1909) contends that the original Gospel by John Mark uses mainly Peter's reminiscences, but holds that a redactor has enlarged and revised the whole under Pauline influences. Hence he tries to get back to the "original" Mark. But this effort has met with a poor reception from modern scholars. Bacon's attempt to give us the "Petrine Christ" of the original Mark in contrast with the "redactor's Christ" of our present Mark is confronted with Peter's own picture of Christ in 1 Peter, even if we, for the sake of argument, leave to one side 2 Peter. Then we have Peter's speeches in Acts as reported by Luke. Schweitzer ridicules the outcome thus: "Modern historical theology, therefore, with its three quarters scepticism, is left at last with only a torn and tattered Gospel of Mark in its hands" (*Quest of the Historical Jesus,* tr. 1910, p. 307). Schweitzer is himself a free lance, with vagaries enough of his own concerning eschatology as the sole key to Christ's teaching, but he is pitiless in his arraignment of "liberal" German theology which has overthrown "the Gospel of Mark as an historical source" because they could not get rid of the deity of Christ in Mark as it stands. "The literal Jesus has given place to the Germanic Jesus." "So at the present day the Germanic spirit is making a Jesus after its own likeness." Schweitzer is himself a German, and wrote some years before the war began. What would he now say about "the good German God" of the war literature?

Mark in Harmony With the Other Evangelists

The truth is, that the whole tone of Mark's Gospel, the earliest of the Gospels, is precisely that of the other Gospels and of the rest of the New Testament. "The beginning of the Gospel of Jesus Christ, the Son of God." So the book begins. It is immaterial whether we take the first verse as part of the Gospel or the "headline" as Swete suggests. It is a true description of the book. Some manuscripts do not have "the Son of God," but the Gospel has it. Mark is giving us, therefore, the story of the beginning of the good news of Jesus Christ, the Son of God. So much emphasis has been laid on the fact of the beginning that some have overlooked the fact that

Mark presents Jesus as the Christ the Son of God. But he does so all through his book.

The humanity of Jesus is in the second Gospel without peradventure. Mark makes no effort to reconcile the human traits of Jesus with His deity. He draws the picture sharply and boldly as Peter did in his preaching. Let us go through the Gospel rapidly and note the marks of Christ's deity which are present.

At the baptism of Jesus the Spirit rests on Him, and the Father greets Him as His Son. "Thou art my beloved Son, in thee I am well pleased" (Mark 1:11). Peter probably heard John the Baptist, who was present, tell of this voice from heaven. But at any rate, Mark's Gospel here at the very start proclaims Jesus as the Son of God in a sense not true of other men, in the Johannine sense of deity on a par with the Holy Spirit. In reality the doctrine of the Trinity is contained in 1: 9-11 in Mark's concrete fashion. He states the facts and leaves us to draw our conclusions from them.

The demoniacs hail Jesus as the "Holy One of God" (1:24), and Jesus does not repudiate the description, though he bids them hold their peace. "And the unclean spirits, whensoever they beheld him, fell down before him and cried, saying, 'Thou art the Son of God'" (3:11). Did Jesus deny that He was the Son of God? Far from it. He admitted it. "And he charged them much that they should not make him known" (3:12). He thus confessed His deity and Mark means us so to understand Jesus. It was not a disclaimer, but a prohibition against revealing Him in His true character. So the wild man of the tombs cried out: "What have I to do with thee, Jesus, Thou Son of the Most High God?" (5:7).

The disciples accepted Jesus as the Messiah early, but did not of course fully comprehend His deity. Indeed, not till the bestowal of the Holy Spirit at Pentecost after the resurrection of Jesus did they understand that Jesus was not the political Messiah of Pharisaic theology, for just before his ascension they reveal the failure to grasp the conception of the spiritual kingdom: "Lord, dost thou at this time restore the kingdom to Israel?" (Acts 1:6). In Mark's Gospel we see the growing wonder of the disciples themselves as they see the power of Christ over wind and wave, while Jesus upbraided their lack of faith. "And they feared exceedingly, and said one to another, Who then is this, that even the wind and the sea obey him?" (Mark 4:41). When they saw Him walking on the water "they were sore amazed in themselves" (6:51).

The people have various ideas about Jesus. Some follow the lead of the Baptist and take Him as the Messiah, though Jesus avoids that term for awhile to prevent political complications. Others consider Him Elijah or one of the prophets, while Herod Antipas fears that Jesus is John the Baptist risen from the dead (6:14f).

Christ's Claim of Equality With God

The exercise of the power to forgive sins was understood by the enemies of Jesus (the Pharisees) to be a claim of equality with God and to be blasphemy: "He blasphemeth: who can forgive sins but one, even God?" (2:7). Jesus did not disclaim being equal with God as they thought. On the contrary, He proceeded to heal the man to show that He did have authority to forgive sins and so was equal with God, "that ye may know that the Son of man hath authority on earth to forgive sins" (2:10). Certainly Mark puts Christ in the light of making a claim of deity by this act and by His words of defense. The use of "the Son of man" by Jesus in no way contradicts this position, for Jesus loved to refer to Himself by this Messianic title, which in itself places Him above man while partaking fully of human nature, for as the Son of man Jesus is the representative man, the ideal man, more than any other man.

In the Transfiguration scene, Jesus is again specifically addressed by God as His Son: "This is my beloved Son: hear ye Him" (9:7). Certainly this tremendous experience presents Jesus in the light of the Son of God. Moses and Elijah came back to pay homage to Jesus and to converse with him. Jesus on the way down the mountain refers to Himself as "the Son of man," though the voice from heaven had just addressed Him as the Son of God. Even if one seeks to explain away the historical character of the Transfiguration, the fact remains that Mark's Gospel presents Jesus as divine on this occasion as at His baptism. The testimony of the demons has been discounted by some because of the source, but here it is the Father Himself who speaks. The witness to Jesus as the Son of God is given from heaven and from hell.

Schmiedel makes a good deal of the disclaimer of Jesus in 10:18: "Why callest thou me good? none is good, save one, even God." He makes this one of His nine "pillars" which cannot be shaken, because no disciple of Jesus would invent a saying which so clearly denies Christ's own deity. Schmiedel says that he has been misunderstood, and claims that he does not mean that Jesus did not say other things, but that these cannot be disproved. At least we gain thus proof that Jesus actually lived, if one is in need of that evidence. But it is by no means clear that Jesus means to deny His deity by the question to the rich young ruler who rather lightly had called Jesus "good teacher." Jesus took him up on the word "good" (Greek, *agathos*), which in its absolute sense can be applied only to the perfectly good, that is, God. Jesus does not say that he is not good in that sense. He opens the way for the young man to define himself in his attitude towards Jesus. When he spoke to Jesus again, he said "teacher" (10: 20). And he was not willing to follow Jesus at the cost demanded of him.

His Enemies Understood Him

In the triumphal entry Jesus allowed himself to be proclaimed the Messiah and planned the entry as a formal proclamation of his Messiahship (11:1-10). In the parable of the husbandmen and the vineyard Jesus makes it plain that He is the beloved Son whom they slew, and the enemies of Christ so understood Him (12:1-12).

Jesus claims to be David's Son and David's Lord to the confusion of His adversaries. He evidently meant by this use of Psalm 110 to claim deity for Himself as well as humanity (12:35-37).

In the great eschatological discourse (chap. 13) on the Mount of Olives Jesus refers to Himself as the Son of man coming in clouds with great power and glory" (13:26), coming as Judge of all the earth. But he also says that He is "the Son" in relation to "the Father," a distinct claim to deity (13: 32). In this very verse He mentions the fact that He does not know the time of His second coming, but this limitation can in no way offset the direct claim to being the Son of God in antithesis as in John's Gospel.

Mark makes no attempt to reconcile the deity of Christ with His humanity, as John does through his Logos doctrine. Jesus is in the closest fellowship with His Father. In the agony in Gethsemane he appeals to His Father as "Abba, Father" (14:36), using both the Aramaic and the Greek words as Paul does in Romans 8:15. He and the Father were so completely at one that He felt the shock of the withdrawal of the Father's face as He hung on the cross, the sacrifice for human sin. Thus we are to understand the cry of utter desolation from the heart of Christ: "My God, my God, why hast thou forsaken me?" (15: 34). This cry proves Christ's humanity, but does not disprove His deity. It was the first time that Jesus had ever felt the loneliness of momentary desertion by His Father. Nothing shows us the blackness of our sin more than this cry of Jesus from His bleeding heart. He had apparently faced all other problems connected with His death save this. Or at any rate He did not know till it came to pass how hard it would be to be looked upon as sin (2 Cor. 5: 21): "Him who knew no sin he made to be sin on our behalf." This was the sorest part of all the tragedy of the Cross. But may we not say that the Father, like any other Father, suffered also in that hour when the Son bore the penalty of the world's sin?

Even in His death Jesus showed His deity when the Roman centurion exclaimed, as he saw Him die: "Truly this man was the Son of God" (15: 39). It is not clear how much the centurion meant by the phrase. The way that he spoke it can be translated "a son of God" as in the margin of the Revised Version. The inscriptions and papyri show us how lightly people of that time used the term "God." They worshipped the Roman Emperor and called him "god," and set up statues of him to be adored. In a very real sense the Christians challenged the Roman Empire by their worship of Jesus. Soon the issue was that of Christ or Cæsar. Paul felt it in his day. "No man speaking in the Spirit of God saith, Jesus is anathema; and no man can say, Jesus is Lord, but in the Holy Spirit" (1 Cor. 12:3). Polycarp was given the alternative, Cæsar or Christ. He was asked to say "Lord Cæsar," but he replied each time, "Lord Jesus." So he died for his fidelity to Jesus as Lord.

The Sanhedrin put Jesus to death, but He rose from the grave, as Mark shows (16:1-8). The grave could not hold Him. With Mark's Gospel alone we could face the world with the gospel of the Lord Jesus Christ the Son of God.

Chapter III

THE CHRIST OF MATTHEW'S GOSPEL

It is still disputed among scholars whether the Apostle Matthew is the author of our Greek Gospel of Matthew. It seems reasonably clear that the Logia which Papias said that Matthew wrote in Hebrew (Aramaic) was the non-Markan document common to both our Matthew and Luke. Both Matthew and Luke made use of Mark, as any one can see for himself by the careful study of a harmony of the Gospels. The picture of Jesus drawn in the Logia of Matthew is our earliest known portrait of the Saviour. That by Mark (due to Simon Peter) is the second. Both of these we still possess, for we can see the outline of the Christ of the Logia by following the non-Markan portions of Matthew and Luke in any harmony of the Gospels. We have also the picture of Christ in Luke's Gospel, drawn by the great Christian painter and physician, and that in John's Gospel. We have, moreover, that in our Greek Matthew which blends the elements in the Logia of Matthew and in Mark. It is not a mere mechanical copy, but the interpretation of a great soul for a high purpose on a par with that of John in the Fourth Gospel. For our purpose it is not necessary to decide who is the author of the Greek Matthew, though there is no sound reason why the Apostle Matthew himself may not have written it, making use of his own Logia, of Peter's Memoirs of Jesus (Mark's Gospel), and of his own rich experience and notes. He was a business man and used to keeping data and may have made full notes during the ministry of Jesus. If he wrote the Logia in Aramaic for the early Jewish Christians of Palestine, he may have written our Gospel in Greek for the Jewish Christians of the Dispersion. But our problem now is to see what sort of a picture of Jesus is furnished us in the Greek Matthew as we have it.

The book is probably the most useful one ever written, because it comes first in the New Testament collection and has done more than any other to create the impression of Jesus that the world has obtained. It is the most widely circulated through the ages and the best known. The author has a thesis and writes to prove that Jesus of Nazareth is the Messiah of Jewish prophecy and hope. Schuerer says that the two nerve centers of Judaism were love of the law and the Messianic hope. They were both grounded in the Old Testament. Hence the Gospel of Matthew has more Old Testament quotations than any other Gospel. The Jewish love of the law became the bondage of the letter that was the death of the spirit. The rabbis "bind heavy burdens and grievous to be borne, and lay them on men's shoulders; but they themselves will not move them with their finger" (Matt. 23:4). The Gospel of Matthew shows that Jesus is superior as a teacher of righteousness not only to the legalistic rabbis, but even to the Old Testament sages and prophets (Matt. 5), for Jesus will carry the meaning of the law to the deeper impulses and intent of the heart while He frees men from the bondage of mere ceremonialism and legal technicalities. In Matthew Jesus is pictured as saying in contrast to the Old Testament, "But I say unto you" (Matt. 5:22, 28, 32, 34, 39, 44).

He took the moral law seriously and aimed to make it effective and to uncover the hypocrisy of the Scribes and Pharisees. Hypocrite was His terrible word for those who hindered men from finding God and truth and life and righteousness. The Sermon on the Mount is still the highest ethical note struck by any teacher in all time and is to-day considered impractical and idealistic by some business men and politicians who find it difficult to square their practices with the type of righteousness here set forth. It is not merely higher than that of the Scribes and Pharisees of that day, but it is higher than that of any day. Jesus denounced in withering terms the hypocrisy of the perfunctory religious teachers of the day, as reported in Matthew 23 (see my "*The Pharisees and Jesus,*" for exposition of the chapter), but he gave a positive ethical program for the individual and for mankind.

Jesus claimed to be the great interpreter of God in Matthew as in John. The famous passage in Matthew 11:25-30 (Luke 10:21-24) is thoroughly Johannine and greatly puzzles those critics who argue that the Fourth Gospel is responsible for the type of teaching here found, where "the Father" and "the Son" are shown to be in full fellowship in a fashion not true of others. The Gospel of Matthew was probably written before the destruction of Jerusalem and John's Gospel about 90 to 95 A.D. Jesus in this passage in Matthew invites men to come to him for expert knowledge of God as he does in John 5. He is here the great Teacher. The Gospel of Matthew lays special emphasis on the teaching of Jesus, and this passage is the core of it all. Jesus is the Teacher of God. The Son alone fully knows the Father, and the Father alone fully knows the Son.

But the Messianic hope had become perverted like the love of the law. The promise of the Messiah runs through the Old Testament with varying degrees of clearness. It is by no means certain that the prophets themselves always saw that the Messiah was to be King in a spiritual Zion and not a political king in Jerusalem. They sought to understand what the Spirit of Christ in them did testify (1 Pet. 1:10-12), but their gaze was far away as they saluted the promises in the dim future (Heb. 11:13, 39). The persecutions of the Jews at the hands of many masters revived the Messianic hope as their one chance of deliverance from oppression. In particular, Antiochus Epiphanes stirred the Jews to long for the coming of the Messiah, who would throw off his yoke. In the time of Christ it was the Roman tyranny that stimulated hope of a deliverer. It was unpopular to pay tribute to Cæsar (Matt. 22:17). When Jesus came, his life and claims were interpreted by the people in the light of this hope. The excited crowds looked for a revolution against Rome such as the Zealots started about A.D. 65, which led to the destruction of the city and temple in A.D. 70.

The Messianic hopes of the people found utterance in numerous Jewish apocalypses that claimed to unveil the future by showing the downfall of the enemies of the Jews, particularly the Romans, and the establishment of a world-wide Jewish kingdom, but the language used was largely cryptic and known only to the initiated. It was not safe to express one's ideas about Rome too plainly. So this type of eschatological teaching took the apocalyptic form. We have in the Apocalypse of John the great Christian example of it. The hopes of the people varied and many were grotesque and excited. Second Esdras (Fourth Ezra) in the Apocrypha is a good specimen of it as is the Book of Enoch which is part Jewish and part Christian. The apocalyptists make popular a theological language of symbolism about the kingdom. Elements of this type of teaching appear already in Joel, Ezekiel, Daniel. Peter applied the language of Joel to what took place on the great day of Pentecost, and affords us a good example of how the apocalyptic symbols about "blood, fire, and vapor of smoke" were applied to spiritual experiences (Acts 2:17-24). The Gospel of Matthew reports Jesus as making considerable use of the apocalyptic symbolism in his teaching of the kingdom of God, particularly in the eschatological aspects of it (Matt. 24, 25).

But it is quite beside the mark to say, as Schweitzer does, that Jesus preached only in eschatological terms and had no ethical element in his teaching and had no world program. The very proportion of things in the Gospel of Matthew disproves this notion. The Sermon on the Mount (Matt. 5-7) is meant for the present life, not for the life in heaven. Jesus gave the Great Commission with a program for world conquest (Matt. 28:18-20). The parables of the Kingdom in Matthew 13 show that Jesus looked for the slow growth of the Kingdom, like the mustard seed to the full shrub, like the leaven spreading through the meal; with varied results, like the seed of the sower on different soils; with a world struggle between the forces of good and of evil in the world, like the wheat and the tares in the same field (the world) with final separation only at the harvest at the end. To then Matthew's Gospel presents Jesus as the Great Teacher of the Kingdom of Heaven that has already come, that is in the heart and that is the pearl of great price, that reaches into all the phases of our complex life on earth, that is meant to make earth like heaven, where the will of God is done, with individual and social regeneration, with the choice of a chosen band of leaders who are to carry on the work of teaching and healing of soul and body to the ends of the earth.

Matthew's Gospel thus limns the true Messiah (the Christ, the Anointed One, Matt. 1:1, 16; 16:16) against a background of misapprehension and of perversion. He represents Jesus as employing the current eschatological terminology (Matt. 24-25) about the consummation of the Kingdom in language that is mingled with a discussion of his own death, the destruction of Jerusalem, and the end of the world. But the eschatological is a minor note in the teaching of Jesus. He repeatedly says that we do not know when the end will come and so must be ready to greet the Lord when He comes (Matt. 25). He will come in His own good time, that is clear. We must "watch." But we are not to sit idly by and let evil run riot with the world. We are to busy ourselves with Christ's great world program, the missionary propaganda, as seen to-day in evangelical Christianity. Herein rests the whole case for the evangelistic and educational program of Christianity (our churches, Sunday schools, colleges, newspapers, books).

But Matthew's Gospel undertakes to show that, while Jesus did not fulfill the current Pharisaic expectation of the Messiah, he did realize the Old

Testament outline of the Jewish Messiah. He shows that Jesus is the son of David, and so could be the Messiah (Matt. 1:1, 6, 17, etc.) He is in the Messianic line. He is also the son of Abraham (Matt. 1: 1, 2, 17), the father of Israel. In the genealogy Matthew seems to give that of Joseph through whom the legal genealogy of Jesus would run, not the actual genealogy of Jesus through Mary, as in Luke. Matthew's Gospel means to say that the royal dignity of David, which was lost in the captivity (Matt. 1:11) was restored in Jesus (1:16). In the Triumphal Entry, Jesus was hailed as the Son of David and as King (21:9, 15). At the time the people believed that Jesus would really set up the Davidic Kingdom in Jerusalem, but Matthew knows now in his Gospel that Jesus is a spiritual King. We must not forget that Matthew records the Great Commission, which includes all the nations. Certainly Jesus did not mean that the Gentile Christians were to become Jews, but that point was already clear when Matthew wrote.

But how does Matthew prove that Jesus is the Messiah of Jewish promise and hope? Josephus tells of many false Messiahs who gained a following and then dropped away. Jesus himself tells in Matthew 24 of false Christs (Messiahs) who will lead astray, if possible, the very elect. In our own time we have seen multitudes led astray by false teachers (men and women) who have set themselves up as substitutes for Jesus Christ. Not all the people who saw and heard Jesus accepted him as Messiah and Saviour. But some did and the first to do so were Jews. Matthew writes specifically to convince other Jews that Jesus is in reality the Christ. His line of argument is not difficult to follow.

He shows that Jesus fulfilled the Old Testament requirements for the Messiah not merely in the matter of his Jewish descent and Davidic lineage. These quotations are not all prophetic predictions in the sense that the prophet intended them to be Messianic. Some of them are illustrations of Scripture as shown in the providence of God. Thus Matthew draws a parallel between the life of Jesus and the Old Testament to show the Messianic dignity of Jesus. Isaiah foretold the birth of Jesus, the Messiah (Matt. 1:22-23); Micah had said it would be at Bethlehem (Matt. 2:6); Jeremiah gave a parallel to the slaughter of the babes (2:17, 18); Hosea pictured the return of the child Jesus from Egypt (2:15); a prophet dimly sketched the settlement at Nazareth (2:23); Isaiah outlined the coming of the Forerunner (3:3), the ministry of healing (8:17), and the avoidance of publicity (12:17-21); the Psalmist pictured the preaching in parables (13:35), while Isaiah explained why the people could not understand them (13:14-15); Zachariah described the Triumphal Entry into Jerusalem (21:4-5); Jeremiah (Zechariah) foretold the price set upon the life of Christ, while Jonah was a type of the three days in the tomb (12:40). This presentation would have undoubted influence with those familiar with the Old Testament. Some of the quotations are from the Hebrew and some from the Septuagint. Some are in the words of Jesus, while others are in the narrative of the author. This use of the Old Testament at times approached the mystical method of Philo occasionally found in Paul's Epistles and was a common one among the rabbis.

Matthew not simply calls Jesus the Son of David in a Messianic sense, and the Christ, but he shows (1:21) that his very name Jesus (Joshua) was given because of his redemptive work as the Saviour from sin. He is to be another Joshua, to deliver Israel, not from the people of Palestine, who confronted Joshua, and not from the Roman tyranny, but from the thraldom of sin. He is to be the world's deliverer from sin and sickness and sorrow, and to bring Salvation to mankind.

The favorite term in the mouth of Jesus in Matthew to describe his own claims is the Son of man. The phrase is in Ezekiel to emphasize his own humanity. Daniel has it in an apparent Messianic sense (Dan. 7:13 ; 10:16, 18). But the Book of Enoch is full of it, though it is not certain that all of it is before the time of Christ. An effort has been made to show that in the Gospels Jesus merely meant to call himself "a man" by the use of "the Son of Man," like the Aramaic *barnasha*. But many passages in the Gospels utterly refuse that sense, which would be mere affectation on the part of Christ or gross mistranslation on the part of the writers of the Gospels in rendering the Aramaic. And certainly the high priest understood Jesus to make a Messianic claim by the use of the term "the Son of man" (Matt. 26:64), and by Jesus as tantamount to "the Christ, the Son of God," in the question of the high priest (26:63).

Besides, the people in Jerusalem identify "the Christ" with "the Son of man," and wish to know "who is this Son of man" who is to be "lifted up" instead of abiding forever (John 12:34). It is plain that the phrase was in popular use for the Messiah, and yet it was not the technical language of the rabbis. Hence Jesus used it commonly in order to make a practical Messianic claim and yet at the same time to avoid giving his enemies a technical charge against him. There was, moreover, another advantage in the phrase. It expressed finely the real humanity of Jesus and he loved to put emphasis on that fact. He was a real man, not a mere phantom. But he was also the representative man, the ideal man, the goal of humanity, the hope of the race. Mark has the phrase fourteen times, while Matthew uses it thirty-three.

But in Matthew Jesus is also the Son of God just as truly as in the Gospel of John. It is involved in Matthew's report of the Virgin Birth of Jesus. The Sinaitic Syriac Manuscript reads in 1:16 that "Joseph begat Jesus," but that same manuscript leaves the language unchanged in 1:18-25, where Joseph was about to put away Mary because he was not the father of her child soon to be born. Evidently, therefore, the text has been tampered with in 1:16 or "begat" is not used in the literal sense. None of the uncial Greek manuscripts have this reading, though the Ferrar Group of minuscules do support. Matthew's testimony cannot be turned against the Virgin Birth of Jesus. In 1:20 Joseph is told to take Mary, "for that which is conceived in her is of the Holy Spirit." This conception of the actual deity and actual humanity of Jesus runs all through the Gospel. The Magi worship the child who is born the King of the Jews (2:2, 11). At the Baptism of Jesus the Father addressed him as "My beloved Son" (3:17). In the temptations, the devil takes up this language at the baptism, and undertakes to suggest to Jesus how to prove that he is a "Son of God" (4:3, 6). The wild Gerasene demoniac hails Jesus as "Thou Son of God" (8:29). In the famous passage, 11:25-30, Jesus speaks of himself as "the Son" of "the Father," in a sense not true of other men. This unique relation constitutes the only ground of his appeal to men to come to him to learn of God. In 14:33 the disciples worship Jesus in the boat as "the Son of God." In 16:16, in response to the question of Jesus to the disciples, Peter pointedly confesses their faith in him as "the Christ [the Messiah], the Son of the living

God." At the transfiguration the Father again addresses Jesus as "My beloved Son" (17:5). In 26:63 the high priest formally put Jesus on oath to say if he claimed to be "the Christ, the Son of God," and Jesus said: "Thou hast said" (26:64), that is, "Yes," or "I am," as Mark has it (14:62). As Jesus hung on the cross, the rabble mocked him for claiming to be "the Son of God" (27:40) and the rulers also reminded him of his claim (27:43). A Roman centurion was so much impressed by the death of Jesus that he said: "Truly this was God's Son" (27:54). When Jesus stood on the mountain in Galilee and gave the Great Commission to more than five hundred, he sent them forth to make disciples and to baptize "in the name of the Father and of the Son and of the Holy Spirit" (28:19). This verse has been attacked on the ground of being too Trinitarian and too ecclesiastical. But Matthew's Gospel is Trinitarian throughout and Jesus held himself to be the Son of God by the testimony of the Logia, of Mark, of Luke, of John, and of Matthew. The testimony cannot be rejected on that ground. Jesus meant his language, not as a formula to be followed *verbatim,* but as a crisp interpretation of the theology of the plan of redemption. The Father, Son, and Spirit are all involved in the redemptive work and in the Gospel propaganda.

So the Gospel of Matthew closes with the majestic scene on the mountain in Galilee, where the risen Christ announces his program for world conquest, by which he is to fulfil his claim to be the Jewish Messiah and the world's Saviour. It is not a conquest by the sword. Jesus has no army. It is not a rule by state authority. Jesus was put to death by the combination of ecclesiastical and civil rulers. Christianity will have to fight for its life with the Roman state. The Kingdom of Heaven will grapple with the Kingdom of the World, with Cæsar's kingdom, in a way to justify the vague fears of Pilate. But it will be an unequal struggle at first. Without human power, without money, without culture, without organization, this band of believers is charged with world conquest. Here is sublime faith, sublime audacity, sublime optimism. It seemed like a wild Utopian dream. But to-day the centuries justify Matthew's picture of Jesus. The greatest force in human history is not Moses, not Caiaphas, not Alexander, not Plato, not Cæsar, not Napoleon, not Shakespeare. Jesus has moulded human history as no other man has or will. He is the Lord of Glory to-day and the Lord of life. He is the world's hope and guiding star. He is the only Saviour from sin.

Matthew drew the picture of the Messiah for the Jews. But they have rejected their own Messiah, as John's Gospel so tragically shows. But the Christ of Matthew is the Christ of the race and we can all follow the Magi to the Babe in Bethlehem and the women to the Cross and to the empty tomb and to the mount of destiny and service. The call of the Christ echoes to-day over the centuries. The nations cry piteously to us for help. Jesus is the answer to their cry. He has promised to be with us to the end. In Matthew, Jesus is often represented as promising to come again to earth. The early Christians were cheered by this blessed hope. So must we look for his coming again with joy in his own good time.

CHAPTER IV

LUKE'S PICTURE OF JESUS

It is probable that Luke never saw Jesus in the flesh. The tradition that he was one of the Greeks (John 12:20) who came to Philip at the last passover in Christ's ministry has no foundation in fact. It is inconsistent with the implication of Luke 1:2 that Luke himself was not one of the "eye-witnesses." We have the picture of eye-witnesses in Matthew's Logia, if not his Gospel, in Peter's Memoirs of Jesus (Mark's Gospel), and in the Fourth Gospel (John's Portrait of Christ). These men were all Jewish Christians of Palestine of the first generation. But Luke is a Greek Christian of Syria and Macedonia who learns of Jesus from those who knew him in person. He is a scientist and a man of the culture of the schools. Tradition says that he was a painter, but he was certainly a physician and a historian of great gifts of industry and of style. He applied himself methodically to the task of gathering and digesting information about Jesus from first-hand sources both oral and written (see my *Luke the Historian in the Light of Research*).

Naturally, therefore, Luke's Gospel shows a marked contrast in the purely Jewish phases of

Christ's life to that of Matthew. There is no unusual effort to prove that the Old Testament prophecies were fulfilled in the life of Jesus, though that element is not wanting. Luke himself shows knowledge of the Septuagint in various ways and was influenced by the style of the Septuagint here and there. In his genealogy he does not stop with Abraham, but goes back to Adam and evidently cares more for the universal aspect of Christ's humanity than for the fact that he was a Jew. In his report of the Sermon on the Mount Luke omits the contrast between the teaching of Jesus and that of the Scribes and Pharisees. So also he does not give the fierce denunciation of the Pharisees as we have it in Matthew 23.

Luke gives much that is original in comparison with the other Gospels, fresh material that he probably secured while in Palestine during Paul's imprisonment in Cæsarea (chiefly in chapters 9 to 19). The wonderful parables in chapters 12, 14, 15-18 come in this section of his Gospel. To be sure, these are the parables of Jesus, the foremost story-teller of all times, but Luke has recorded them with consummate literary skill. He has an eye for an effective setting for each picture or parable as it comes. His Gospel is a series of pen pictures of Christ. The great story is unrolled like a panorama before us. It is nowhere overdone. Often we could wish for more, but it is plain that the author has used a critical taste in his selection that must be respected. In all literature no story surpasses in sheer beauty and charm that in Luke 24.

Luke begins with the Wondrous Child. Here he is in touch with Jewish sources, probably partly oral and partly written, which he translated from the Aramaic. He writes in chapters 1 and 2 with delicate sympathy and genuine faith of the great mystery of the Virgin Birth. The standpoint is that of Mary and ultimately came from her either through intimate friends or directly from her to Luke. The Christian physician shows the utmost care to put Mary right before the world which already had more than vague whispers about the birth of the Child Jesus. The faith of this intelligent physician in the supernatural birth of Jesus, his real deity and real humanity, lifts the narrative above the plane of legend and old wives' fables. Luke makes no attempt to explain the mystery and the miracle. But science cannot say to God how far he can and cannot go in the working of his will. At best science is only an effort to understand those of God's laws that it can bring within the radius of human intelligence. He is a poor scientist who dares to affirm positively what is beyond that realm. And science acknowledges parthenogenesis in the lower forms of life. But Luke tells, also, of Mary's own wistful searchings of heart and soaring of soul under her great experience. He tells of the angel Gabriel and the song of the heavenly host and of the manger in the place for the cattle. Like a true historian he locates the place and time of the birth of Jesus (Luke 2:1-7) in language that once aroused the scorn of critics, but that now challenges their admiration as stone and papyrus have vindicated every detail in the narative (see my *Luke the Historian*). Luke tells, also, how the Babe grew in stature and in wisdom, grew also in favor with God and man. And Luke alone breaks the silence of the thirty years after the return to Nazareth from Egypt till the sudden appearance of the Messiah by the Jordan before the Baptist. The Boy Jesus, now twelve years of age, in the temple in Jerusalem reveals to Joseph and Mary a consciousness of his Messianic mission when he speaks of his duty in his Father's house (Luke 2:49). This single glimpse into the heart of the growing Boy shows that Mary had already begun to see the fulfilment of her hopes and dreams about her wondrous son. But at the same time she does not quite understand the change that is coming in the Boy Jesus as he turns toward his destiny. Does any mother, in truth?

Luke now gives us the Conscious Christ. The years pass by! The Carpenter in Nazareth hears of the stirrings by the Jordan. The people were wondering if John were not himself the Christ (Luke 3:15). John disclaimed that office, but pointed out that the real Messiah was at hand. One day he came. John had looked wistfully into the face of every man as he baptized him and watched for the sign that had been promised by which he could recognize him (John 1:33). But when John and Jesus stood face to face beside the Jordan, the Baptist recognized the Messiah at once before the sign, but the sign came after the baptism and the Father's voice of approval of the Son was heard by the Baptist (Luke 3:21-22). The Son knows that the Father wills for him to enter his Messianic Mission. Besides, the Holy Spirit rests upon him always. The Trinity meet at the baptism of the Son. Jesus is in no doubt about his task as he enters upon it. In the temptations the devil subtly challenges the words of the Father, to the Son and proposes how the matter may be put to the test to prove if in reality Jesus is the Son of God. This presentation comes ultimately from Jesus himself and refutes the view that Jesus only took the notion of being the Messiah toward the close of his ministry as a gradual discovery when he saw how eager the people were for the Coming One. The Synoptic Gospels show that at the baptism and temptations Jesus is as fully conscious of his redemptive work as in John's Gospel. Besides, in the first visit at Nazareth Luke pictures Jesus identifying himself with the Messiah of Isaiah's roll (Luke 4:16-30) to the mystification and to the final fury of his fellow townsmen who actually seek to kill him for his presumption. But Jesus goes on to Capernaum which is to be his new home in Galilee and the center of the campaign to win Galilee to recognition of his claims to be the Messiah. But he had found in Jerusalem how hostile the Pharisees were and they will watch his work in Galilee so that Jesus avoids the public use of the term Messiah which the masses accepted in a political sense.

Luke pictures Jesus the Great Physician and evidently does it *con amore*. He had worked with Paul and had seen Paul heal the sick by the power of Christ while Luke himself practised the medical art. Undoubtedly the miracles of Paul which he witnessed predisposed him to believe the miracles wrought by Jesus. In his Gospels, as in the Acts, Luke reveals a natural fondness for medical terms and in particular he loved to bring out the features in a narrative that appealed to the doctor. So he tells more miracles of healing the sick than any other writer and takes pains not to reflect on the work of the physician in so doing. The pity and compassion of Jesus for the sick and the suffering met a deep response in the heart of Luke. No true physician can see all the pain and anguish about him without wishing to relieve it. The medical missionary of to-day is doing a work like that of Luke and, also, like that of Jesus. "And as ye go, preach, saying, The Kingdom of heaven is at hand. Heal the sick, raise the dead, cleanse lepers, cast out demons. As a gift ye received, as a gift impart" (Luke 10:7-8). These words to the Twelve as they went on their tour of Galiiee interpret Christ's will for men to-day. Jesus did not teach opposition to physicians, but he urged prayer to God along with use of the physician.

In Luke's Gospel we see Jesus as the Popular Preacher. The crowds come and go in great throngs. They press upon him so that people climb upon the housetop and into a tree as Zaccheus did. But Jesus loved the people. His heart went out to them in compassion and he blessed the feeblest faith that sought to touch even the hem of his garment. He healed when power went out of him as it always goes out of those who give themselves to the heavy-laden. But Jesus was not merely the Wonder Worker. As John Foster has said, his miracles were like ringing the bells of the universe to draw attention to the sermon that was to follow. "The multitude welcomed him, for all were waiting for him" (Luke 8:40). They gathered sometimes "in tens of thousands, so that they trod upon one another" (Luke 12:1). But Jesus grew weary of the mere crowds and longed for the kindling of the fire of his death, the baptism of his blood (Luke 12:49, 50). Once he turned upon the great crowds and announced hard terms of discipleship to sift the mere hangers-on. But Jesus was the friend of the poor and even of the outcasts of society. He let the publicans and the sinners draw near to him even when that fact led to sharp criticism from the Pharisees and the Scribes (Luke 15:1, 2). The Master defended himself in his mission to the lost in the peerless parables of the lost sheep, the lost coin, the lost son.

So Luke paints Jesus as the Challenger of Tradition. The Pharisees perceived that Jesus was undermining their system of teaching. They early began to criticize his usurpation of divine authority in forgiving sins. They soon began to accuse him of being in league with the devil. They call him a common Sabbath-breaker. They clash with Jesus over fasting and over association with the sinners. Even the Pharisees who invited Jesus to their homes criticize him so that Jesus has to expose their hypocrisy for taking away the key of knowledge themselves and hindering those who wished to enter (Luke 11:52). The tension was keen and the sympathy of Luke is wholly with Jesus.

Luke shows Jesus to be the Man of Prayer. At the baptism, on the Mount of Transfiguration, in the Garden of Gethsemane, on the Cross Jesus prayed. The disciples noticed his habit of prayer and asked to be taught to pray. He would spend whole nights in prayer as before choosing the twelve disciples. One must believe that Luke himself was a man of prayer as some physicians are known to be. Luke does not picture Jesus as an unreal man with no need of finding God in prayer. All the more, because he is the Son of God, he seeks fellowship with the Father, knowing that the Father understood him. The more men misunderstood and plotted against him the more he found refuge in the Father's love and sympathy.

Luke represents Jesus also as the Champion of Women and Children. He tells of the woman who followed Christ in the tour of Galilee. He shows that Jesus found a home in Bethany with Martha and Mary. He gives the supreme picture of Mary the Mother of Jesus and he alone tells of Elizabeth and Anna. The good physician understands women who tell him many of their secret sorrows and woes.

In Luke's Gospel Jesus is the Compassionate Priest. In the very act of dying on the Cross for the sin of the world Luke represents him as saying: "Father, forgive them; for they know not what they do" (Luke 23:34). And he saved the repentant robber while dying and said: "To-day thou shalt be with me in Paradise" (Luke 23:43). Love can go no further. Luke does not argue formally the doctrines of the faith, but he gives the concrete expression of the gospel message in a way that all can comprehend. In Luke the gospel is universal and inclusive of all who will let Christ reign in the heart as King and Saviour.

Once more Luke portrays Christ as the Risen Lord. If he had written nothing else, the twenty-fourth chapter would have made his Gospel immortal. But that wonderful picture of the Stranger revealing himself to the two despondent disciples on the way to Emmaus comes at the close of the great Gospel narrative. It is the climax of a series of narratives set in a frame like pastels side by side. The cumulative effect is overpowering. Jesus is the Risen King of Glory here and forever. The disciples now rejoice as they leave Olivet for the temple. They know now beyond peradventure that Jesus is the Saviour of the world. They have seen him go up on high. But they know that he will come back again. He has promised to give them power from on high with which to win the world to Christ.

CHAPTER V

JOHN'S PORTRAIT OF CHRIST

I

By the caption to this chapter I pin my faith to the conviction that the Apostle John is identical with the Beloved Disciple mentioned in the Fourth Gospel as the author of the book (John 21:20, 24). The Johannine problem is apparently no nearer solution to-day than it was a hundred years ago. The debate proceeds among scholars with undiminished energy, as one can see in James Drummond's *An Inquiry into the Character and Authorship of the Fourth Gospel* (1904), an able defense of the Johannine authorship; William Sanday's *The Criticism of the Fourth Gospel* (1905), in which the whole case is surveyed and the probability thrown in favor of the Johannine authorship; B. W. Bacon's incisive, *The Fourth Gospel in Research and Debate* (1910), in which the Johannine authorship is denied and ably attacked; Garvie's *The Beloved Disciple* (1922), an able argument for a triple authorship; Burney's *Aramaic Origin of the Fourth Gospel* (1922), which plausibly pleads for the Aramaic original. These modern books present the whole case as it now stands. Bacon is as aggressive against the Johannine authorship as if Ezra Abbot, Dods, Drummond, Godet, Lightfoot, Luthardt, Sanday, Stanton, Watkins, B. Weiss, Westcott, and Zahn, had not produced their powerful bulwarks in defense of the Apostle John as the author of the Fourth Gospel. Drummond holds the Johannine authorship is proven, but hesitates at the historicity of the miracles, in particular the raising of Lazarus from the dead. Sanday admits the possibility as an alternative that the Beloved Disciple was not John, but an unknown disciple on as intimate terms with Jesus as John the Apostle. This theory of Delff has attracted some minds as a way out of the critical tangle. Unfortunately, however, his hypothesis makes the Fourth Gospel ignore the Apostle John from indifference or dislike, and puts the unknown disciple in where the Synoptic Gospels and Acts put John as the companion of Peter. I do not propose in this chapter to discuss the problems of the author of the Fourth Gospel, but simply state it here as an introduction to the discussion. Dom Chapman in *John the Presbyter and the Fourth Gospel* (1911) contends with plausibility that the so-called "Presbyter John" of Papias is simply the Apostle John, who calls himself "the Elder" or "the Presbyter" in 2 John 1. *Per contra*, James Moffatt, in his able *Introduction to the Literature of the New Testament* (1911), claims all the Johannine writings for this Presbyter John of the second century. Others, like Harnack and Wendt, attribute the Fourth Gospel to a Johannine school. But the external evidence strongly reënforces the internal arguments for the Johannine authorship. Irenæus expressly says that John wrote the Fourth Gospel, and appeals to Polycarp as the disciple of John and his own friend. Tatian, Justin Martyr, Ignatius, strengthen this explicit testimony, and narrow the date of the Gospel to the last decade of the first or the first decade of the second century. Here we must leave the matter. Each man will make up his own mind in the light of the facts as he sees them. Probability is the law of evidence in all human affairs. There are undoubted difficulties in holding to the Johannine authorship, but my mind sees far more in any other course. So I hold with reasonable confidence to this position, and make no further apology for my title.

II

We have the picture of Christ in the Fourth Gospel as a fact, whoever was the author, and this fact calls for explanation and interpretation. The problem to which this chapter addresses itself is to look at this picture with open eyes and mind alert to all the facts just as they are. Some men have better eyes than others, though the blind preacher George Matheson puts most of us to shame in his study of *St. John's Portrait of Christ* (1910).

The insight of Matheson makes ample atonement for the loss of his eyesight. He had the eyes of his heart enlightened (Eph. 1:18) as he gazed at this picture of Jesus Christ. The glory of a picture is not fully perceived unless one has an eye for beauty and a mind trained by study of technique to appreciate the purpose of the artist and a heart responsive to highest ideals of art. If this is not true, the picture may seem a daub of paint splashed on canvas. It is proper to criticize a picture if one is qualified to do so. We must not be hypersensitive about criticism, even if the critic seems to lack the spirit of reverence and to forget that in the Gospel of John he stands in the Holy of Holies of the Person of Christ. We must listen to what all the critics say, else we may be charged with obscurantism and unwillingness to accept new light. Certainly no one can justly say that the Fourth Gospel has been neglected by the critics. Every verse in it has been subjected to the most scathing criticism of scholarship for over a hundred years. This is a matter for gratitude. We want to know all that is true, whether it is palatable to our predilections and prejudices or not. Only we wish to know that the new is true. Let the scribe bring out of his treasure things new and old. The old is not true because it is old, nor the new untrue because it is new. The only way to get at the truth is to try the spirits. We must criticize the critics. There is nothing infallible about modern criticism any more than about the old. There will never come a time when Biblical scholarship can shirk the duty of working over old issues raised afresh by research or speculation. Men will think and learn, and ought to do so. We make progress by continually challenging the old and then challenging the challenge of the new. Only the truth can stand this sifting, but it is the grain of wheat that we desire for bread, not the chaff. So, then, let us take a frank look at John's Gospel, keeping in mind the searching criticism of modern scholarship.

III

One of the first facts that confronts us is that this Gospel seems so different from the Synoptic Gospels. This is true both of the form and of the contents of the book. The style of the discourses of Jesus is so unlike that of Jesus in the Synoptic Gospels that some critics bluntly say that they cannot both be true. So Bacon says: "Either Synoptics or John. . . . Both views cannot be true, and to a very large extent it is the science of literary and historical criticism which must decide between them. We agree, then, with Bishop Lightfoot that the Johannine authorship of the Fourth Gospel is the question of all questions in all the domain of Biblical science."[1] Now we cannot brush aside this criticism of Bacon without looking at it. One of the best ways to answer a

[1] "The Fourth Gospel in Research and Debate," page 3.

critic is to listen to another critic. E. F. Scott, like Bacon, rejects the Johannine authorship of the Fourth Gospel,[2] and yet he says: "Its dependence on the Synoptics is naturally most apparent in the narrative portion of John's work. He sets before us the same general picture of Jesus as a teacher, a worker of miracles, a Master surrounded by disciples who only half understood him. The conception of the character of Jesus, heightened though it is by the dominant idea of the Logos, is yet essentially the same as in the earlier evangelists. These large features of resemblance do not necessarily imply a direct borrowing, but there are further similarities which cannot otherwise be explained."[3] Scott says "John" simply for convenience, but he stoutly opposes Bacon's exaggerated contrast between the Fourth Gospel and the Synoptic Gospels. There are differences beyond a doubt, but they do not affect the essential framework of the picture. At bottom the two pictures are the same, the same as in Q or the Logia, as a matter of fact. We cannot apply the "Jesus or Christ" controversy[4] to the Gospels and make the Synoptics (or at any rate Q) present "Jesus" and John's Gospel "Christ." Unfortunately for that theory the historical Jesus with his humanity is as vivid in John's Gospel as in the Synoptics, and the

[2] Cf. page 4 of Scott's "The Historical and Religious Value of the Fourth Gospel": "The author of this Gospel was not the Apostle John."

[3] Scott, "The Fourth Gospel, Its Purpose and Theology," 1906, page 33.

[4] Cf. *Hibbert Journal* Supplement, reprint for January, 1909.

Messianic aspect (the Christ) is as plain in the Synoptics (even Q) as in the Fourth Gospel. The differences in the two pictures are in tone, touch, shading, emphasis, not in essence. They do not alter the identity of the picture. They belong to the realm of personality and temperament. It is clear that John's nature responded more quickly, and that he treasured more tenaciously certain aspects of Christ's character. He wrote his Gospel after the others, and probably with full knowledge of what they contained. He planned his Gospel to be a complement and supplement, not a mere contradiction, to the Synoptics. This is shown to be the fact by the material in John's Gospel, which is all new save the Feeding of the Five Thousand and some of the events of Passion Week. His purpose in doing this I shall discuss presently, but the fact is apparent. Besides, it so happens that the characteristic Johannine strain or type of teaching, the very language one may say, appears in a few passages in the Synoptic Gospels. See Matthew 11:25-30; Luke 10:21-24; Matthew 28:18-20. In these famous logia of Jesus we have the Johannine note in indisputable form and substance. We are therefore forced to admit the reality of this style of teaching in the primitive traditions (even in Q, Matthew, and Luke). It is not the invention of the Fourth Gospel, though chiefly preserved there. We have precisely the same problem presented in the teaching of Socrates as preserved by

Xenophon and Plato. Both may very well be true in a many-sided man like Socrates, though the personal equation has entered into both reports. It is uncritical and unscholarly to reject John's picture of Christ because of the special emphasis which he has made upon certain aspects of Christ's life and teaching.

IV

But we are told that in John we have an incarnation without real humanity, while in the Synoptics the historical Jesus is at most deified. "But one must have failed to grasp even the elements of Johannine thought not to realize that this verse (John 1:14) is absolutely central to the system. Incarnation is its keynote."[5] "And yet the older, simpler Christology *has* survived. Neither the teachings as restored from the non-Markan material common to Matthew and Luke, nor the Markan narrative, nor our canonical first or third evangelist, has introduced anywhere one trace of the Pauline doctrine of the preëxistence of Christ or of incarnation. . . . Such is the Synoptic story of Jesus. Its keynote is not incarnation, but apotheosis."[6] The denial of "one trace" of preëxistence is a pretty strong statement. In reply one is justified in referring to the Messianic consciousness as early as twelve years old when the boy Jesus speaks of "My Father's

[5] Bacon, "The Fourth Gospel in Research and Debate," page 7.
[6] *Ibid.*, pages 10f.

house" (Luke 2:50); to the words of the Father at the baptism of Jesus, "my beloved Son," and the presence of the Holy Spirit, the three Persons of the Trinity (Mark 1:10f.); to the words of the devil who assumed his divine sonship while tempting him (Matt. 4:4); to his claim to have the power to forgive sins and so to be God (Mark 2:7-11); to the implication of the demoniac that Jesus as the Holy One of God had come from the other world (Mark 1:24f.; 5:7); to the interview with Moses and Elijah on the mount of Transfiguration and the glory of that occasion (Mark 9:2f.; Matt. 17: 2f.; Luke 9:29f.); to the claim of complete knowledge of the Father (Matt. 11:27); to the claim of power equal to that of God (Matt. 28:18-20). It is not a matter of verbiage, but of fact. It is not consonant with mere human experience for a man to speak as Jesus is represented in these passages in the Synoptic Gospel. The only adequate explanation of these passages is the implication behind the whole story, expanded in John's Gospel and Paul's Epistles, that Jesus is the Son of God incarnate. The story of the Virgin Birth, told by Matthew (1: 18-25) and Luke (1: 26-38), confirms the consciousness of Jesus in the Synoptics and the statement of the incarnation in John 1: 14. Hence we come back to the point that in the Synoptics and in John's Gospel we have Jesus described both as the Son of God and the Son of man. The effort to explain "the Son of man" as merely "man" because of the ambiguity in the Aramaic *barnasha* has not succeeded,[7] for in some passages the point in the expression turns on the representative character of Christ. There are many passages where "the Son of Man" is the judge of men (cf. Mark 8:38; Matt. 16:28). It is in the Synoptic Gospels that Peter's confession of Jesus as the Messiah the Son of God occurs (Matt. 16:16), and that Jesus confesses on oath before Caiaphas and the Sanhedrin that he is the Son of God (Matt. 26:63 f.; Mark 14:61 f.). So, then, this imaginary gulf between John and the Synoptics disappears upon close examination.

V

But it is charged against John that he has written history with a purpose, while the Synoptics give an objective historical picture of Jesus. John does announce his purpose in 20:31: "But these are written, that ye may believe that Jesus is the Christ, the Son of God; and that believing ye may have life in his name." Scott puts it thus: "The narrative is composed with the set intention of proving that Jesus is the Christ, the Son of God."[8] This he says to the discredit of the Fourth Gospel as veracious history. On the contrary, Scott describes the Synoptic story: "This fidelity to the Synoptic traditions was undoubtedly the chief aim of the Synoptic writers. Their work may here and there bear

[7] Cf. Abbott's portly tome, "The Son of Man."
[8] "The Fourth Gospel, Its Purpose and Theology," pages 1f.

traces of theological coloring, but their first interest was with the facts. Their part was not to interpret, but simply to record, as clearly and faithfully as they might, the actual events on which the new religion was based. John, on the other hand, starts with a certain conception of the Person and life of Christ, and records the facts in the light of it. They are valuable to him only as they afford evidence and illustration of a given belief."[9] I have here let Professor Scott have the floor long enough to put his view clearly. It is clever, and has a specious sound as if it might be true. And yet it would be difficult to make more wrong implications in a few sentences. The Synoptic Gospels do not make a dry objective statement of historical events like the Saxon chronicle or a Church calendar. No history worth reading is written in that style. Every historian worth the name after having his facts has an interpretation of his facts, else he has no readers. The true historian gives us his philosophy of history. This is true of Herodotus, Thucydides, Livy, Gibbon, Green, Macaulay, Ferrero. It is true also of Mark, the most objective of the Gospels, for the very works of Jesus show him to be the Christ the Son of God and Son of man. He wrote to impress the Roman world, and told his story with vivid touches from the eye and tongue of Peter. It is true of Matthew, whose Gospel is a manifest apologetic to convince Jewish

[9] *Ibid.*, page 2.

readers that Jesus of Nazareth is in reality the Jewish Messiah of promise. It is true of Luke, the cultured Greek, who mentions his research and care for historical accuracy (1:1-4) after the manner of Thucydides, for no Gospel presents Jesus with more beauty, sympathy, and love as the Saviour for all the lost of all races, the hope and joy of all who feel the need of forgiveness of sin. It is utterly inadequate to say that the Synoptic Gospels are simply neutral monographs like a census report. In simple truth all the Gospels use the facts recorded "with a set intention." Such a use of facts does not *per se* distort the facts. Scott charges John with adapting and modifying his material according to his prepossession, so that the result is perversion of the truth. This is the gist of the whole matter. Bacon (*op. cit.*, pages 5-35) realizes the seriousness of this accusation against John's veracity: "Acceptance of the critical view of the Fourth Gospel involves a great challenge and a great responsibility. There will be no longer the apostolic authority of an eyewitness, a confidant of Jesus' inmost consciousness. Still less will it be possible to present the Christology of the fourth evangelist as the personal testimony of Jesus to himself." I submit that this charge against John is not proven. We have seen that at bottom the picture of Christ in all four Gospels is the same. They all begin and end with the same high conception of the Person of Christ.

They all show the failure of the disciples to understand correctly what sort of a Messiah Jesus claimed to be—a spiritual Messiah, not a political King as a rival to Cæsar. They all show the growth in the manifestation of Jesus, the slow training of the Twelve, the rapid development of hostility on the part of the Jewish leaders till the climax on the cross. But it nowhere appears that John vitiates his report by special pleading, while the Synoptics are disinterested reporters of what they behold. There is in all of them the same worshipful reverence for Jesus as the Son of God, the Redeemer from sin.

VI

But it is further said that John's report is shown to be mere invention because he uses the same style in the narrative portion and in the addresses of Jesus. "He employed stories for his own ends," says Von Soden,[10] who says also that his teachings have been changed "into the theological and philosophical language of the schools."[11] Keim says: "Jesus himself has become the subtlest dogmatician."[12] Jülicher puts it thus: "Jesus must have spoken just as the Synoptists make him speak";[13] and he adds this: "A Jesus who preached alternately in the manner of the Sermon on the Mount and of John

[10] "Early Christian Literature," page 396.
[11] *Ibid.*, page 441.
[12] "Jesus von Nazara," page 112.
[13] "Introduction to the New Testament," page 372.

xiv.-xvii. is a psychological impossibility; the distinction between the so-called exoteric and esoteric teaching a palpable absurdity."[14] Once more, Jackson says: "His individuality is impressed on all his reports of the sayings and discourses of Jesus. The language is his own. It follows that the Fourth Gospel is not throughout a depository of the very words of Jesus as originally spoken."[15] This is enough to present this acute criticism which many feel who admit the Johannine authorship. Stevens, for instance, says: "We must therefore attribute the language, the color, and the form of these Johannine discourses to the Evangelist. The Gospel of John is a distillation of the life and teaching of Jesus from the alembic of the Apostle's own mind."[16] There is an element of truth in this last statement, but the same thing is true of the Synoptic Gospels. Jesus spoke often in Aramaic, and his words are then translated into Greek, and not always by the same word in different Gospels. Besides, in the Synoptic reports of the discourses of Jesus there is an element of freedom which has to be considered. As to the impossibility of the same man speaking in such a different style, we have Paul's Epistles, Shakespeare's plays, Milton's poems, as illustrations of variety in the same person's style. We have seen that both Matthew (11:25-30; 28:18-20) and Luke (10:21-24) have

[14] *Ibid.*, page 421.
[15] "The Fourth Gospel," 1906, page 151.
[16] "Thelogy of the New Testament," page 172.

preserved specimens of this very Johannine style that present a problem quite apart from the Gospel of John. As to John using the same style in the narrative and the discourses, it is quite possible that the style of Jesus has influenced John quite as much as he has modified the language of Jesus. Some natures are more susceptible and retentive than others. I know a man who can repeat almost any sermon that impresses him for months and years afterwards with the tones and emphasis of the speaker. Jesus seems to have stamped his words on John's retentive mind. But it is not necessary to deny that from his mellow memory John to some extent expressed his report in his own language with no injury to the veracity of his account. This is true of all who report extended conversations. But I am not willing to say with Scott that "these discourses appear to be composed freely, according to the method employed in the narrative proper. Words actually uttered by Jesus are expanded and interpreted."[17] In other words, the writer of the Fourth Gospel is simply a dramatist like Shakespeare, who has taken a minimum of fact and has made a maximum of imaginary narrative and conversation. There is dramatic power in the Fourth Gospel, but it is the energy of life as told with the utmost directness and simplicity, not the power of a literary artist. Indeed, nowhere is Jesus set

[17] "The Fourth Gospel, Its Purpose and Theology," page 3.

forth with so much clearness and power as in this Gospel. The writer undoubtedly has the reflective turn of mind natural to an old man, and it is not always easy to separate his own observations from the words of the speakers; but the picture as a whole stands out with marvelous distinctness and startling power and vividness. It is a pleasure to call attention to Askwith's *Historical Value of the Fourth Gospel* (1910), a book that weighs the whole problem with great fairness and ability and justifies John's manner and method as an interpreter of Christ. John's Gospel has stood the test of time and of experience. Christians of all ages turn to this Gospel for the real Christ of comfort and of conflict, the conqueror over the ills of life and the terror of death.

VII

But many stumble over the Logos doctrine which confronts them in the Prologue (1:1-18). It is boldly said to be a wholesale surrender to Hellenism and a hindrance, not a help, to the modern man in his effort to comprehend the historic Jesus Christ. Bacon conceives that John's Gospel gets its Logos doctrine directly from Paul's Epistles: "The roots of the Johannine Logos doctrine are only to a slight and subordinate degree in Philo. They run back by way of Hebrews, and more especially by way of the great Pauline Epistles of the second period, Colossians and Ephesians, through purely Christian soil, to the common ancestor, the Wisdom of Solomon." (*Op. cit.,* page 7.) He traces the whole Christology of the Fourth Gospel as "a straightforward development of the incarnation doctrine of Paul." Bacon asks (*op. cit.,* page 4): "Is the conception of the life of Jesus as an incarnation of the divine Logos a development of Pauline speculation about Christ; or is it Jesus' own teaching about himself?" That is a false alternative. There is no reason to suppose that Jesus called himself "the Logos," nor is it necessary to connect John's teaching specifically with Paul or Philo, though surely that would have been no harm. At any rate, we cannot agree that John's use of the Logos is to be condemned by the phrase "Pauline speculation." Paul called it "revelation." Dr. J. Rendel Harris has shown in *The Prologue to John's Gospel* (1917) that the Prologue of John's Gospel about the Logos has many points of similarity in language and ideas with Proverbs 8:22-30 concerning Wisdom. Paul called Jesus the Wisdom of God (1 Cor. 1:31). It is quite possible that this idea is almost wholly Jewish, as it comes to John with a touch of the Stoic usage in the Wisdom of Solomon. But what boots it all? There has been entirely too much made out of the whole matter. Scott, for instance, says: "There can be little doubt that by thus importing the doctrine of the Logos into the Gospel record, John is not only compelled to do violence to historical fact, but empties the life of Christ of much of its real worth and grandeur, while seeming to enhance it."[18] Again he says (page 175): "The doctrine of the Logos, born of philosophical theory, has nothing to do with the historical revelation in Jesus, and is wholly inadequate to explain it." It is very easy to make emphatic statements like that. As a matter of fact, no single term covers all that is true of "the historical revelation in Jesus." Son of God does not do it, nor Son of man. Certainly Messiah does not do it, nor prophet nor priest nor king, though Jesus is all of these. He is also Redeemer, Saviour, Mediator. If Jesus is God's Only, begotten Son, he has a cosmic relation (cf. Col. 1:15-17; Heb. 1:2 f.) which John describes by the term Logos. John by no means wishes us to understand that this term covers all the aspects of Christ's character and work. It is one aspect which he pictures by means of a word already in use among Greek philosophers, the Stoics in particular, as well as in Hellenistic Jewish writings (like the Wisdom of Solomon and Philo). But already the Jews themselves had their own Wisdom literature (cf. Proverbs and Wisdom of Jesus Son of Sirach), in which Wisdom was personified as the Logos was among the Stoics. In the old Testament also *Memra* (Word) was personified. The double idea of Reason and Speech suited well John's purpose. But we must

[18] "The Fourth Gospel, Its Purpose and Theology," page 173.

beware of the common fallacy of reading into John's language the ideas of Plato or of Philo. We must allow John the right to put his own content into his own language, for at bottom language is only a series of pictures more or less dim and obscure. But surely John was perfectly justifiable in applying the Logos idea of the Old Testament and of Greek philosophy to one side of Christ's nature, as much so as Matthew's Gospel in proving that Jesus was the Jewish Messiah. Harnack[19] argues that the Prologue is merely a philosophical introduction to please a coterie of the more learned, and that it plays no part in the rest of the volume. It is true that the word Logos is not used elsewhere in the Fourth Gospel, but the idea underlies the argument of the whole book. The Prologue is a real introduction to the progress of the thought. John shows this by the constant use of "life" and "light" in the Gospel. He alone uses the word Logos about Christ elsewhere (cf. 1 John 1:1; Rev. 19:13). Philosophy is continually changing its language and its ideas as it endeavors to explain the nature of the universe. John in no sense commits himself to Platonism, Stoicism, Philonism, or Gnosticism, by taking a word, first used in a personal sense by Heraclitus five hundred years B.C., and applying it to the eternal aspects of Christ's Person and work. He has

[19] "Ueber das Verhältniss des Prologs des vierten Evangeliums zum ganzen Werk," 1892.

made a perfectly intelligible interpretation of Jesus as the Incarnate Word of God, the Expression of the Image of God to men as the Son is the Expression of the Father.

VIII

It is further charged against the Fourth Gospel that the book is distinctly sacramental and mystical. It is openly alleged that in John 6:53 the author makes Jesus refer by anticipation to the sacrament of the Lord's Supper: "Except ye eat the flesh of the Son of man, and drink his blood, ye have not life in yourselves." This whole passage about Jesus as the Bread from heaven is undoubtedly mystical. In verse 57 Jesus says: "So he that eateth me, he also shall live because of me." It is here that we see the symbolism of the language. It is spiritual appropriation of Christ, not the literal observance of a sacrament. The mystical strain in the Fourth Gospel is a fact beyond any doubt, but it is not a mechanical imitation of Jewish ceremonialism or of the Oriental mystery-religions. Mithraism had its *taurobolium* or blood-path (in the bull's blood), and redemption by mystic union with the gods was a heathen doctrine. But an extreme like this is no more likely in John's writings than in Paul's Epistles.[20] There is a good discussion of the true mysticism of the Fourth Gospel in

[20] Cf. Kennedy, "St. Paul and the Mystery-Religions."

Watson's *The Mysticism of St. John's Gospel* (1916), the Hulsean Lectures for 1915-1916. There the balance is well kept between contemplation and activity, between formalism and spirituality. John's mysticism is intensely practical. The spiritual and eternal Gospel is the Gospel of life and reality. The believer's union with Christ is vital, not ceremonial. With John, symbolism goes deeper than mere metaphor, but is never mechanical and wooden. The most difficult verse to explain satisfactorily in this connection is John 3:5, "born of water and the Spirit." On the surface it looks as if Jesus is referring to baptism in order to help Nicodemus understand the spiritual nature of the new birth. If so, he cannot mean to teach that baptism is essential to the new birth, because it is not mentioned in verse 3 nor in verse 7. Nicodemus was a Pharisaic ceremonialist, and Jesus apparently put the symbol of the new birth before him in order to help him to comprehend this fundamental step in the kingdom of God. In no one of the Gospels is it made plainer than in John's Gospel that an impassable gulf existed between Jesus and the ceremonialists of the Jewish religion who resented fiercely the freedom and iconoclasm of Christ.

IX

There are other criticisms of the Fourth Gospel that can only be mentioned. The Synoptics give mainly the Galilean ministry outside of Passion Week, while the Fourth Gospel gives mainly the Judean ministry outside of part of chapter 2, chapters 4 and 6. This is true, but it in no sense discredits either narrative if John means to supplement the story. The differences of style between the Fourth Gospel and the Apocalypse have been variously explained. Some see here absolute proof of difference of authorship. One school of critics makes John the Apostle the author of the Apocalypse, and the Presbyter John the author of the Gospel. Another reverses the argument. Some who hold to the Johannine authorship date the Apocalypse early because of its crudities in Greek idiom.[1] *Per contra,* it may be argued that the Apocalypse represents John's style in its unrevised form and when under a certain amount of excitement. We know that John and Peter were considered "unlearned and ignorant men" (Acts 4:13) by the Sanhedrin. They were not schoolmen like Paul. The variations from the literary style seen in the Apocalypse are current in the vernacular[2] κοινή. The raising of Lazarus from the dead is given only in the Fourth Gospel, and forms a stumbling-block to some modern scholars. The Synoptics have the raising of Jairus' daughter and the son of the widow of Nain. But John's Gospel makes so much of the case of Lazarus as

[1] Cf. Moulton's "Prolegomena," page 9.
[2] Cf. Robertson, "Grammar of the Greek New Testament," pages 133-137.

really the occasion of the climax of Jewish hatred and as the immediate excuse for the determination to put Jesus to death. It is argued that so important an item would not have been overlooked by the Synoptic Gospels. But then, if Lazarus was still alive when the Synoptic Gospels were written, they may have passed it by on purpose, since the Jewish authorities tried to kill Lazarus also (John 12:10). It is urged that there is no growth in John's picture of Christ; that he starts as God and ends as God. It is certainly true that the divine element is purposely made prominent in John's Gospel, but there is development all through the book. Jesus reveals himself more and more, and his enemies grow in hatred. Jesus hungers, is weary, suffers, sympathizes, battles with sin and error, dies, rises again, in this Gospel as in the others. But one thing is certain: We cannot draw a sharp line between the Christ of the Synoptics as Man and the Christ of the Fourth Gospel as God. Both elements are in each picture. The mixing of the tints is different, but the features are essentially the same.

The best way to read the Gospels is to begin with Mark's simple description of Jesus the Power of God. Then read Matthew's account of Jesus the Messiah of promise. Then read Luke's portrayal of Jesus the Saviour of the whole world, irrespective of race or sex or rank. Finally, read John's portrait of the Eternal Christ, the

Incarnate Logos, the Son of God and King of Glory. The scene changes, but the Person is the same. We look at Jesus all the time. A different guide has interpreted Christ, but it is the One Jesus Christ, the same yesterday, today, and forever.

X

But if we leave the critics and let John's Gospel tell us of Christ, we shall walk in the high places of the Spirit. With masterful skill John pictures the Baptist bearing witness to Jesus as the Lamb of God and the Son of God. Two of the Baptist's disciples follow Jesus to his abode in Bethany beyond Jordan, one of them the author of the book, and the other Andrew. Each of them brings his brother to Jesus as the Discovery of the ages. The heavenly panorama of the kingdom of God has begun on earth. John's pen-pictures of striking personalities are very wonderful. Andrew, Peter, Philip, Nathanael, Nicodemus, the Woman at the Well, the Courier from Capernaum, the Man Born Blind, the Bethany Family, Mary Magdalene, Joseph of Arimathea, are portraits of undying glory in this wondrous gallery. John reveals Christ in a special way by his relation to each of these. But the greatest thing in the Fourth Gospel is the unbosoming of Christ's own heart in the precious chapters 14-17. Here the tenderness of Jesus with his puzzled disciples reveals the death of his love and sympathy. Thousands through the ages have fed their souls upon Christ's words here recorded. Men and women have lived by these words, and have died with them upon their lips. The comforting Christ looks upon us here and cheers us in our sorrows and stands by the open door of heaven to welcome us when we die.

Chapter VI

CHRIST'S CLAIMS OF POWER AND KNOWLEDGE

There is no room for doubt about the claim of Jesus to deity, as presented in the Gospel of John. The Jewish leaders openly attacked him on that ground, "because he not only broke the Sabbath, but also called God his own Father, making himself equal with God" (John 5:18). In the apologetic address which follows Jesus defends his right to that claim. Indeed, it is precisely the open advocacy of the deity of Jesus in the Fourth Gospel that makes the book unacceptable in many quarters to-day, though some Trinitarian scholars deny the Johannine authorship and some Unitarian scholars defend it. But at any rate it is urged that the Synoptic picture of Christ is wholly different. Here, it is said, we have the human Jesus, not the heavenly Christ, the Son of God, of the Fourth Gospel and of Paul.

Unfortunately for that theory the facts do not support the contention. This "aerolite from the Johannine heaven" (Hase) does not stand alone. This passage in Matt. 11:25-29 may be compared with Luke 10:21-24. If not from the same source, then a widely scattered and early tradition supports it (Allen). Besides, the same type of teaching appears in Matt. 28:18-20. Harnack admits the genuineness of the passage in Matt. 11:25-29, though he has attempted a reconstruction of the text on purely speculative grounds. It will not do to interpret the words of Jesus here as a mere claim to special knowledge of God such as every prophet or mystic professes to possess. The words "the Father" and "the Son" forbid that interpretation. The Synoptic gospels have this Johannine phrase elsewhere, as in Mark 13:32; Matt. 24:36. We are in the same atmosphere of seclusive fellowship between the Father and the Son that is so common in the Fourth Gospel, as in 5:19-29 and chapters 14-17. The point is whether in Matt. 11:27 Jesus claims only fuller knowledge of God such as any man may obtain, or fullness of knowledge of the Father possible only to the Son because of his unique relation with the Father as the Son. The latter is undoubtedly the case, and is a claim to deity or equality with God in the Johannine sense. There is no reason to press the words "all authority" in Matt. 28:18, but it obviously means more than "these things" in Matt. 11:25, which were concealed from the wise and prudent and revealed unto babes. Knowledge of God is not a matter of the intellect, but of the heart. Even the simple can know more of God than some of the willful intellectuals who close their hearts to him. But

Jesus possesses full knowledge of the Father. Each knows the other because of identity of nature and life as others cannot know God. The Son alone knows the Father as the Father knows the Son. To be sure, Jesus is not here claiming for himself omniscience about everything. He admits lack of knowledge about the time of his second coming (Mark 13:32; Matt. 24:36). He had undoubted limitations to his knowledge during the incarnation (cf. the emptying of glory in Phil. 2:7), though we are by no means able to set bounds to the knowledge of Jesus in his humanity. He exhibited surprise and disappointment along with undoubted superhuman knowledge. The mystery of the knowledge of Christ is part of the mystery of his nature as the Son of God and the Son of Man. "Jesus is the authorized instructor in the knowledge of God" (Broadus). Here he claims to speak as Master, not because of superior intellectual powers, or because of scholarly research, or because of peculiar piety. He alone is competent to reveal God because of his peculiar relation to the Father. The Son is able to speak out of his own experience with the Father. To be sure, in one sense the Son is not equal to the Father, as Jesus himself says in John 14:28, "for the Father is greater than I." So every true son feels about his father. But the Son stands on a plane of equality with the Father in relation to all others. Moses was faithful as a servant in the house of God, "but

Christ as a son over his house" (Heb. 3:5). In Matt. 11:27 Jesus is speaking as the Son who alone has the right to speak of his Father to those who wish to learn about him. Indeed, the Son claims the power of choice in revealing the Father, "to whomsoever the Son willeth to reveal him." The upshot of it all is that Jesus in Matt. 11:25-29 is in a rhapsody of intimate fellowship with the Father. We can thus form some idea of what prayer was to Jesus when he communed with the Father. He is "in the bosom of the Father" (John 1:18), "God only begotten" (true text), and so "hath declared" (ἐξηγήσατο, cf. our "exegesis," "interpretation," "revelation") God.

We need not make too much of the Greek tenses here. The aorist παρεδόθη may refer to a definite experience in the human life of Jesus. But it can very well be the timeless or gnomic aorist (cf. my *Grammar of the Greek New Testament in the Light of Historical Research*, pp. 836 f.), expressing the state of Christ's consciousness in his relation with the Father. Certainly this saying of Christ "bears the stamp of superhuman consciousness" (Meyer). Jesus is fully conscious that he is entrusted with the task of teaching men the knowledge of God by reason of his peculiar relation with the Father as the Son. It is the same idea that we meet in John 14:9, when Jesus said to Philip, "Have I been so long with you, and dost thou not know me, Philip? He that hath seen me hath seen the Father: how sayest thou, show me the Father?" The unique knowledge about God that Jesus possesses is due to the filial relation, not to mere bestowal or revelation as to prophets and sages. It is in this sense that Jesus claims equality with God, the equality of the Son's fellowship with the Father.

Let us now turn to Matt. 28:18, where Jesus asserts the possession of all power: "All authority hath been given me in heaven and on earth." No mere man in his senses could make this astounding claim. In Matt. 11:27 Jesus is quoted as saying: "All things have been delivered (παρεδόθη) unto me of my Father." Here the verb is likewise in the aorist tense (ἐδόθη), which also may be the timeless aorist, or refer to a definite experience in past time. If the latter, one may think of the councils of eternity or of some event in time like the incarnation or the Messianic consciousness of Jesus. Dalman holds that Judaism has never known anything of preëxistence of the Messiah antecedent to his birth as a human being, but Allen (*Matthew*, pp. 122 f.) shows that in the Jewish apocalypses such preëxistence is recognized. This point is not material. What is pertinent is that "Jesus claims universal authority" (Broadus), "limitless" (McNeile), "free from all limitation" (Meyer). The word here is not power (δύναμις), but authority (ἐξουσία). It is authority by right of position as God's Son. It is conferred on Christ by the Father whose right it is to bestow it (Rev. 2:27). This word ἐξουσία is very common in the New Testament, and is used in various ways. It is used of universal authority or right also in Jude 25; Rev. 12:10.

We are debarred from placing limitations on the authority of Christ in this passage by the use of "all" and, in particular, by the words "in heaven and on earth." Jesus exercises this authority in perfect harmony with the Father, but it is the sway of God, not of man. "Human thought loses itself in the attempt to understand what must be comprehended in such authority as this. Nothing less than the divine government of the whole universe, and of the kingdom of heaven, has been given to the risen Lord" (Plummer). We are familiar with this teaching about the cosmic Christ in the writings of John and Paul. The point to note is that the Synoptic Gospels present the same essential picture of Jesus. Certainly the authority claimed by Jesus includes all that is needed for his spiritual activities in the work of redemption, but Jesus is presented as the Creator in John 1:3 f., and in Phil. 2:8-10; Col. 1:16 f.; Heb. 1:2. It is a work of supererogation to try to empty the language in Matt. 11:27 and 28:18 of the natural fullness of content called for by the very context. The cry used to be "Back to Christ," with the idea of getting rid of Paul and John. But criticism finds the cosmic Christ in the Synoptic Gospels, even in Mark and in Q. It is not, then, mere man who is charged with a great mission who speaks in Matt. 28:18-20, but the Son of God, victor over death and sin.

The command of Jesus for world-evangelization is the fulfillment of the vision in Daniel 7:14. It is in the fullness of divine authority that Jesus here lays upon the group of early disciples assembled on the mountain in Galilee the task of world-conquest. "He must have supreme and divine dominion who commands eternal life to be promised in his name, the whole world to be reduced under his sway, and a doctrine to be promulgated which is to subdue every high thing and bring low the human race" (Calvin). This mystic conception of world-sway is rendered all the more wonderful when we contemplate the situation of the risen Christ. From the human standpoint he was without resources. He had, it is true, a band of believers, but he was discredited by the Jewish leaders, and had been crucified as an impostor. He had no human government, no army, no money, no schools of learning—nothing with which to carry on a world-wide propaganda. The claim of Christ is humanly preposterous, as the task laid upon his followers seems impossible of achievement. The audacity of it all is magnificent, but the calm unconsciousness of audacity is manifest. Christ never appears more at ease, more natural, than on this sublime occasion when he is laying down his program for world-conquest. He speaks as the Messiah, the Son of God, who is fully equal to the task in which he is engaged, and which he lays upon the disciples. He has at his command "all authority" in heaven and upon earth. Even the disciples are not to be discouraged or faint-hearted. They are to have courage because Christ is Master of the universe. In the execution of the mediatorial work Jesus has full functions (1 Cor. 15:24-28), and he will exercise them till this work is completed. But when that task is accomplished he will still be the Son of God, the Creator and Sustainer of the universe (Col. 1:16 f.). The resurrection of Jesus from the dead after his repeated prediction that he would rise on the third day gave force to his claim to divine prerogative and power as the Son of God. It is a most solemn occasion, and Jesus "announced in the simplest and least ostentatious way the most original, the broadest, the sublimest enterprise that ever human beings have been called upon to accomplish" (Hanna). One must recall the words of the Father to the Son on coming out of the water of baptism: "This is my beloved Son, in whom I am well pleased" (Matt. 3:17, cf. Mark 1:11; Luke 3:22). Jesus has no doubt about that. He has finished the task given him to do on earth. Now, before he ascends to his place by the Father's side in glory he lifts the curtain of the future for the mightiest conflict of the ages. It would be hopeless but for the "all authority" of Christ and for the promise of his daily presence through the ages.

Chapter VII

OUR LORD'S COMMAND TO BAPTIZE

1. *Fresh Interest in the Subject*

One would think that the controversy over Matthew xxviii. 19 had pretty well run its course since F. C. Conybeare (*Zeitsch. für die Neutest. Wissensch.*, 1901, pp. 275 ff.; *The Hibbert Journal*, October, 1902) and Kirsopp Lake (Inaugural Lecture at Leiden, January 27, 1904) argued that the command to baptize in the name of the Father and of the Son and of the Holy Spirit was not a part of the original text in the Gospel of Matthew, but was interpolated for dogmatic reasons (Trinitarian and ecclesiastical) into the text. In particular it was urged that Eusebius gave the true text in the short form: "Go, disciple all the nations in my name." It was pointed out also that nowhere else in the New Testament is the Trinity associated with baptism. The points at issue were thoroughly threshed out and answered by Riggenbach in his *Der Trinitarische Taufbefehl Matth., Beiträge zur Förderung christl. Theol.*, 1903, and in particular by Chase, "The Lord's Command to Baptize" *The Journal of Theological Studies*, July, 1905. To my thinking there was little left of the attack on Matthew xxviii. 19 when Chase was through with it. Maclean (Baptism in *Hastings' Dictionary of the Apostolic Church*) says that the careful refutation of the view of Conybeare and Lake by Riggenbach and Chase "has made his position untenable, and we can with confidence assert that the full text is part of the First Gospel." But Scott in the one volume *Hasting's Dictionary of the Bible* hesitates to appeal to Matthew xxviii. 19 since "the authenticity of this passage has been challenged on historical as well as on textual grounds." In an article in *The Watchman-Examiner,* of New York, January 3, 1918, Dr. H. C. Vedder declares that no one who is "intellectually honest" can affirm that Jesus commanded Baptism in view of the doubt about Matthew xxviii. 19. To do so is to use "the language of either ignorance or dishonesty." Dr. T. H. Bindley has a short note on "The Lord's Command to Baptize" in *The Journal of Theological Studies,* July, 1918, and a luminous paper on "The Original Meaning of Matthew xxviii. 19" in *The Interpreter,* October, 1918. The question is one of more than academic interest. If Jesus did not give any command to baptize, we have still His own example in submitting to baptism at the hands of the Baptist. If it was becoming to Jesus thus to fulfil righteousness, surely those who claim to be His followers cannot easily shirk the same obligation. But it remains true that Jesus did not Himself baptize any one, though His disciples did for a time. After the early months of the ministry in Judea and Samaria we hear no more of baptizing by the disciples of Jesus. But on the great Day of Pentecost Peter suddenly enjoins baptism in the name of Jesus Christ upon all the three thousand converts. And they were baptized. From that day forward baptism regularly follows confession and faith as in the ministry of John the Baptist. It is too much to say that without the command of Jesus in Matthew xxviii. 19 the Christian is free from any obligation to follow the Lord in baptism. But it is equally clear that the Lord's command to baptize, as an integral part of the Great Commission, has been a tremendous force upon the consciences of those who follow Him as Lord and Saviour. One cannot view with unconcern the effort to discredit this passage that has been one of the battle cries of Christendom through the ages. But neither does a modern Christian desire to be the pious dupe of an ecclesiastical formula which is foreign to the mind of Christ. Obscurantism has no place in the program of enlightened Christianity to-day. No verse of the New Testament can be held if it is a mere fetish or a magic charm. If Matthew xxviii. 19 has to go, let it go. Only one wishes to be quite sure that this great Logion of Jesus must go to the scrap-heap before he throws it out. To my way of thinking the argument of Plummer on this passage in his really great commentary on Matthew is conclusive. But let us look at the facts.

2. Is It a Genuine Part of Matthew's Gospel?

The external evidence for it is absolutely overwhelming. Every known Greek Manuscript of this portion of Matthew, both uncial and cursive, contains the Lord's command to baptize in the name of the Father and of the Son and of the Holy Spirit. Every extant version that has this portion of Matthew has it also. The *Didachè* (7) about A.D. 100 has it with the addition of "in living water." Justin Martyr (A.D. 150-160) gives it (*Apol.* i. 61). The text of Matthew is further given by the Doctrine of Addai (Burkitt, *Evangelion da-Mepharresche,* i. 173; 153), by Irenaeus (*Lat.* III. xvii. 1), and three times by Eusebius (*Ep. Caes.; c. Marc. Anc.,* i. 1; *Theol. Eccl.,* iii. 5). But elsewhere Eusebius often quotes the passage freely without the command to baptize. The case against the passage, so far as external evidence goes, turns wholly upon the failure of Eusebius always to quote the passage in full. Why did Eusebius vary in this manner? One writer (Dr. Vedder) bluntly says: "The clearest case of this kind is Eusebius who quotes the Great Commission without the clause on baptism." So he does, but he also quotes it with the clause on baptism. Conybeare and Lake argue that the baptismal clause was interpolated for dogmatic reasons and was not in the original text which Eusebius had and usually quoted. At the most, then, Eusebius had two sets of documents, one without the baptismal clause. That, in the abstract, is possible, but in the face of the unanimous testimony of Greek manuscripts, versions, fathers, it must be the only alternative before it gains much force. There is another alternative. The Christian writers quoted freely and only now and then with precision. This is seen in Justin Martyr, for instance. In *Apology* i. 61 the "Threefold Name" occurs in connection with baptism, but in *Trypho* 39 we have "some made disciples in the name of Christ." In the *Didaché* (7) we have the command in full, but in section 9 we find: "But they that have been baptized into the name of the Lord." In the second instance Justin Martyr and the *Didaché* are not quoting, but are simply referring in an abbreviated way to the command. May not Eusebius be doing the same thing? Dr. Samuel Lee (used to good purpose by John Humpstone in *The Watchman-Examiner* for January 31, 1918) in his preliminary dissertation to his translation of the *Theophania* of Eusebius (p. 44) quotes from the Epistle to Cæsarea: "Each one of these we believe to be and exist: the Father, truly the Father; and the Son, truly the Son; and the Holy Ghost, truly the Holy Ghost, even as our Lord, sending forth His disciples to preach, said: 'Go (and) make disciples of all nations baptizing them in the name of the Father and of the Son and of the Holy Ghost.'" Here Eusebius quotes the Lord's command to baptize precisely as we have it in Matthew xxviii. 19, and we can readily see why he quotes it because the passage deals with the Trinity. But in the *Theophania* there is another passage that throws light on the habit of Eusebius: "But He who was their Lord solved by one additional word the aggregate of the things which they doubted, and pledged them by saying, *Ye shall conquer in My name.* For it was not that He commanded them simply to go and make disciples of all nations: but with this excellent addition which He delivered, viz., *In My Name.*" It is evident that Eusebius here is concerned simply with "in the name of the Son," and not, as above, with the name of all the Persons of the Trinity. He uses all or part of the passage as occasion demands, very much as preachers do to-day. Plummer sums up the matter thus: "Eusebius quotes the verse, with the command to baptize into the name of the Trinity, when it suits his purpose; when he requires the rest of the verse, but not the command, he omits the latter." There the matter may be left. Allen (*int. Crit. Com. on Matthew*) regards the testimony from Eusebius as "indecisive." That is surely putting it mildly. But, even so, it makes it out of the question to employ Eusebius as a strong enough lever to overturn the absolutely overwhelming evidence for the genuineness of the passage in Matthew xxviii. 19.

3. But Did Jesus Say It After all?

It is objected further that the passage is under suspicion, even if Matthew wrote it, since it stands alone in the New Testament. Everywhere else in the New Testament baptism is in the name of Jesus. This point seems to have some force when thus presented, and certainly it must be considered. It is argued that the text of Matthew reflects the atmosphere of a later age and simply must have been interpolated on doctrinal grounds, whatever may be true about the usage of Eusebius. It must be remembered that Synoptic Criticism shows that our Greek Matthew must belong to the first century A.D. Ignatius (*Smyrn.*, i.) has an unmistakable reference to Matthew iii. 15 (A.D. 110-115). The *Didaché* (7), as we have seen, quotes Matthew xxviii. 19, or, at least, the same logion of Jesus. Clement of Rome (A.D. 94-6) shows marked similarities with Matthew. McNeile (*Commentary on Matthew,* p. xxvi.) thinks that Matthew and Luke are "quite independent, and neither shows distinct signs of priority." It is possible, though not certain, that Luke knew Matthew (Robinson Smith, *Hibbert Journal,* April 1912). Like Luke, Matthew used both the Logia (Q) and Mark. But Matthew's Gospel seems difficult to place much later than the destruction of Jerusalem (A.D. 70) according to Allen (p. lxxiv.) and Plummer (p. xxxii.). McNeile (p. xxviii.) prefers A.D. 80. The point is not material to our argument. It is clear that Matthew xxviii. 19 comes within the memory of the living tradition of the Sayings of Jesus. We cannot affirm that it was in Q or in Mark. We should know better if we had the real ending of Mark. Allen thinks it quite possible that "the phrase may already have stood in the lost ending of Mark" (p. 306). At any rate "this command is implied in the appendix to Mark" (Plummer, p. 431). Plummer considers it a "reasonable inference" since Mark begins his Gospel with the promise that Jesus would baptize with the Holy Spirit.

The fact that the record in Acts always has baptism in the name of Jesus rather than in the name of the Trinity has no weight unless one takes the view that Jesus meant His command in Matthew xxviii. 19 to be a baptismal formula. Of that we shall speak presently. If it is not meant as a formula, we will have to face the question whether it is in harmony with the standpoint of Jesus and whether it does not represent a later theological and ecclesiastical outlook. Plummer frankly admits the abstract possibility "that, although the Evangelist wrote these words, yet they do not represent anything that our Lord actually uttered; he may be putting into Christ's mouth the baptismal formula, and which he was sure must have Christ authority" (p. 432). This argument proceeds on the basis of the "formula" idea. Plummer pointedly replies that there is too much Trinitarian doctrine in the New Testament not to believe that Christ did say something like this. Paul, for instance, has reference to "the Threefold Name" in 1 Corinthians xii. 4-6; 2 Corinthians xiii. 14; Ephesians iv. 4-6. We see it plainly in 1 Peter i. 2. On this passage Hort says: "How such an idea could arise in the mind of any apostle without sanction from a Word of the Lord, it is difficult to imagine, and this consideration is a sufficient answer to the doubts which have been raised whether Matthew xxviii. 19 may not have been added or recast by a later generation."

As a matter of fact, we have the basis for the doctrine of the Trinity in Mark xiii. 32 in the antithesis between "the Father" and "the Son." It appears also in Q in the like antithesis there (Matt. xi. 25-27; Luke x. 21 f.). There are numerous references to the Holy Spirit in Q and Mark. We cannot rule out Matthew xxviii. 19 on the ground of the Trinitarian teaching, for we find that in Mark and Q, our oldest documents for the life and teaching of Jesus.

McNeile (p. 437) is not certain that Jesus said these words at the point where Matthew has placed them, though convinced that they belong to Matthew's Gospel: "It is probable, not that Matthew's text is unsound, but that the whole clause is due to him, and that the Lord did not *at this point* command the rite of baptism." McNeile, however, adds: "But that He commanded it before His death is in any case extremely probable, since it best accounts for the early and universal use of the rite in the Church." In conclusion McNeile says: "The validity of the rite is far from being annulled if the present passage was not an utterance of the risen Christ." It must be acknowledged that McNeile is hyper-sensitive on this delicate point. He is so anxious to concede every point in all fairness that, though Matthew xxviii. 19 is genuine, we still must concede the possibility that Matthew may have made up the logion or an interpretation of a true word of the Lord. But let the point be granted. We still have to account for the sudden resumption of baptism on such a scale as at Pentecost and with such uniformity thereafter. That situation calls for a command from the Lord Jesus before His Ascension. Matthew xxviii. 19 fits the historical situation in Acts ii. Surely this neat adjustment does not throw suspicion on the passage from the standpoint of historical criticism. Rackham (on Acts ii. 41) thinks that the first edition of Matthew's Gospel (about A.D. 60-70) used the language of that time in reporting the words of Jesus in Matthew xxviii. 19 instead of the original command to baptize in Christ's name. But the constant allusions to the Trinity in the Epistles demand some such command as this to explain them (Bindley, *The Interpreter*, October, 1918, p. 43).

4. But Is It a Baptismal Formula?

Is it necessary to believe that, if the words are a genuine logion of Jesus, He meant them as an "exact form of words to be used in baptism"? It is clear that Jesus "would not prescribe a set form of words for this purpose" (Plummer, p. 433). All modern scholars practically agree that Jesus was unlikely to do such a thing. If the language of Matthew xxviii. 19 is beyond doubt a ritualistic formula, then some doubt may exist as to whether this is after all the teaching of our Lord. Lindsay (*Int. Stand. Bible Encycl.*) calls Matthew xxviii. 19 "the formula of Christian baptism." It is true that Tertullian (*De Bapt.* 13) expressly asserts that in Matthew xxviii. 19 the "law of baptism has been imposed and the formula prescribed." It is trine immersion: "And it is not once only, but thrice, that we are immersed into the Three Persons, at each several mention of Their Names" (*Adv. Praxean.*). There is no doubt that the words of Jesus in Matthew xxviii. 19 came to be used as a formula and gave rise to trine immersion. But the problem is, not later ecclesiastical custom, but the point of our Lord. Did He mean His command to be a set and necessary formula?

It is submitted that this is by no means a necessary interpretation of the language. The fact that the Acts uses only the name of Jesus in connection with baptism shows that no such formula was considered necessary. Peter urges at Pentecost that the new believers "be baptized in the name of Jesus Christ" (Acts ii. 38). Cornelius and the rest were ordered by Peter to "be baptized in the name of the Lord Jesus" (Acts x. 48). The mistaken disciples of the Baptist at Ephesus were "baptized into the name of the Lord Jesus" (Acts xix. 5). Paul spoke of being "baptized into (unto) Christ" (Rom. vi. 3, etc.). Plummer pointedly says: "If our Lord had really given directions that the Trinitarian formula was to be employed by the Apostles, the formula given in Acts would never have come into use" (p. 433). But do we have a "formula" in Acts? The language varies too much to be a "formula." The essential thing was to baptize in the name of Jesus Christ in order to distinguish Christian baptism from Jewish proselyte baptism. We have seen that the *Didaché* and Justin Martyr and Eusebius, all have the short form and the long form. Both undoubtedly existed. By and by the full form was insisted upon as necessary. Cyprian (*Ep.* lxxiii. 18) argues against the practice of baptizing "in the Name of Jesus Christ." The *Apostolical Canons* (50) forbid a presbyter baptizing "into the death of Christ" with "only one immersion which is administered into the death of the Lord." Trine immersion proves the use of the Trinitarian formula. But we do not know that it was so practised at the very beginning. Maclean (*Hastings' Dictionary of the Apostolic Church*) argues that, since "it was our Lord's habit not to make regulations but to establish principles," we may conclude that in Matthew xxviii. 19 "He did not here prescribe a formula, but unfolded the spiritual meaning of the rite." This interpretation coincides best with our Lord's teaching and with the apostolic practice of freedom, while it explains also the later development of the ritualistic formula from the word of the Master.

5. *Shall We Say "In" or "Into?"*

Allen (p. 396) is clear that a distinction is to be drawn between "in the Name of Jesus Christ" (Acts ii. 38; x. 48) and "into the Name of the Lord Jesus" (Acts xix. 5). The one symbolizes the fact that one has become a disciple of Jesus, the other lays stress on the result of the ceremony. Plummer (p. 433) thinks that "baptizing into the Name of the Trinity may mean immersing into the infinite ocean of the Divine Perfection." Both prepositions (ἐν and εἰς) are those justified, he holds, but they convey different ideas. He here follows Heitmüller (*In Namen Jesu*). But, in view of the practical identity of the two prepositions (see Robertson's *Grammar of the Greek New Testament*, p. 592), it is doubtful if a real difference can be insisted upon in Acts. The papyri and the inscriptions give numerous instances of εἰς τὸ ὄνομα where money is placed to the credit of one. The instances in the New Testament are many where one cannot render εἰς by "into" as in Matthew xii. 41: "They repented *at* the preaching of Jonah." And in Matthew x. 41 we have the very idiom εἰς ὄνομα : "He that receives a prophet *in* the name of a prophet," "*in* the name of a righteous man," "*in* the name of a disciple." It is probably an over-refinement, therefore, to contend for "into the Name of" in Matthew xxix. 19. The baptism is commanded by Jesus and is to be performed on the authority of the Trinity. The Name of Jesus alone was enough, for He stood for the Trinity. But the act of baptism rightly symbolizes one's relation to the Trinity, and hence each Name is given by our Lord. In the papyri "name" (ὄνομα) often is used for the person or the authority of the person. It occurs frequently in the Septuagint in this sense. See Acts i. 15: "The number of the names (persons) together were about one hundred and twenty."

We are driven, therefore, by every line of argument to adhere to the Lord's command to baptize as a genuine part of Matthew's Gospel and a true Saying of Jesus. Certainly there is nothing that modern scholarship has brought to light that justifies our setting aside this Magna Charta of the Christian propaganda. The Lord's Command to baptize stands as an integral part of the great Commission. Men differ in their interpretation of it. The spirit of the teaching of Jesus inclines one to take it as a symbol of the new life already begun, not the means by which the change is wrought. In other words we do not have a sacramentarian injunction, but a symbolic picture of the death to sin and the resurrection to life as Paul expounds it in Romans vi. 4. But baptism belongs to the program of Jesus in the evangelization of the nations.

Chapter VIII

THE PRIMACY OF JUDAS ISCARIOT

The Rev. A. Wright has a striking note in the October, 1916, *Journal of Theological Studies* (pp. 32-4) on the question whether Judas Iscariot was "the first of the Twelve." He argues strongly for the idea that Judas was originally the leader among the Twelve, chiefly because of the critical text in Mark xiv. 10: Ἰούδας Ἰσκαριὼθ ὁ εἷς τῶν δώδεκα. There is not much doubt about ὁ belonging here before εἷς, though it is supported only by the Neutral Class of Manuscripts (ℵBC.*vid. LM Cop.). The Western-Alexandrian-Syrian classes do not have the article (DC², the mass of the uncials and the cursives and Origen). D supports εἷς also with ἐκ followed by the Old Latin and Vulgate *unus de* (or *ex*) *duodecim*. The transcriptional evidence is strongly in favor of ὁ εἷς since this is the difficult reading for the scribe. In John vi. 71 the correct reading is εἷς, ἐκ τῶν δώδεκα without ὤν. Intrinsic evidence in Mark xiv. 10 will allow either of the disputed readings, assuming that the author was familiar with the facts in the case. We have, therefore, to explain the reading ὁ εἷς. Alford had long ago accepted this reading, but took the ὁ here as "untranslatable in English: 'that one of the twelve' is too strongly demonstrative; and yet ὁ is demonstrative, and expresses much." Certainly ὁ is sometimes demonstrative in the New Testament as in the older Greek, the original use of this form. Note ὁ μὲν οὕτως, ὁ δὲ οὕτως in 1 Corinthians vii. 7. In James ii. 14 ἡ πίστις would be nearly parallel to this idiom in Mark xiv. 10 ("Can that faith save him?"). The Revised Version takes note of the difficulty by rendering, "he that was one of the twelve" with a marginal note to the effect that the Greek has "the one of the twelve." Klostermann (*Handbuch zum Neuen Testament*) explains ὁ εἷς not as in contrast with ὁ ἕτερος or οἱ λοιποί, but as equivalent to εἷς τις, "der den christlichen Lesern (aus 3 [19]) bekannte." Bruce ignores the point in the *Expositor's Greek Testament* as does Gould in the *International Critical Commentary*. But Swete faces it squarely thus: "ὁ εἷς naturally implies a contrast to ὁ ἕτερος (cf. e.g. Lc. vii. 41, xvii. 34 f.); surely, if it is to stand, the contrast is apparently with οἱ λοιποί, 'that one, the only one, of the Twelve who proved traitor or was capable of the act,' or 'the notorious member of the body,' as opposed to εἷς τις, an unknown individual: unless ὁ εἷς = εἷς ὤν, cf. ὁ εἷς τῶν ἁγίων ἀγγέλων in Enoch xx. ff." Evidently Dr. Swete is unable to make up his mind even to accept ὁ and finds it troublesome, but he does not think of Dr. Wright's solution that ὁ εἷς is here equivalent to ὁ πρῶτος.

The κοινή undoubtedly used ὁ εἷς as an ordinal. In proof Wright refers to Moulton's *Prolegomena,* p. 96. The papyri and the inscriptions support this position. In modern Greek the ordinals above four have disappeared before the cardinals. In the New Testament we have εἰς μίαν τῶν σαββάτων (Matt. xxviii. 1), πρωΐ [τῇ] μιᾷ τῶν σαββάτων (Mark xvi. 2), τῇ μιᾷ τῶν σαββάτων (Luke xxiv. 1; John xx. 1; Acts xx. 7), κατὰ μίαν σαββάτου (1 Cor. xvi. 2). See my *Grammar of the Greek New Testament in the Light of Historical Research,* pp. 671 f. Moulton had already cited from the papyri illustrations of ὁ εἷς *Expositor,* VI. vii. 111). The point may therefore be granted from the linguistic side that in Mark xiv. 10 ὁ εἷς can mean "the first" if the context demands it.

Certainly it is the simplest way to translate it, and there are fewer difficulties of any kind save one. Was not Simon Peter the leader of the Twelve? He came to be at last, and all the four lists of the Twelve begin with Peter (Matt. x. 2 f.; Mark iii. 16 f.; Luke vi. 14 f.; Acts i. 13 f.). Likewise they all end with Judas Iscariot save the list in Acts, which omits him because of his suicide. So far as these lists go the case is decisive for the primacy of Peter and the depreciation of Judas Iscariot. Besides, the angels at the tomb give the woman a message from the Risen Christ in which Peter is singled out: "Go, tell His disciples and Peter" (Mark xvi. 7). On the great Day of Pentecost it is Peter who speaks (Acts ii.) and all through the early chapters of Acts Peter's leadership seems undisputed till the rise of James, the brother of Jesus, and the conversion and activity of Saul of Tarsus. Paul mentions James and Cephas and John as "pillars" in Jerusalem, but he picks out Peter as the Apostle of the circumcision while he himself is the apostle of the uncircumcision (Gal. ii. 7-9). But Paul does not hesitate to rebuke Peter face to face when he cowered before the Judaisers in Antioch (Gal. ii. 11 ff.).

The fact that Peter was one of the inner circle of three in the room at the raising of Jairus' daughter (Mark v. 37) and on the Mount of Transfiguration (Matt. xvii. 1; Mark ix. 2; Luke ix. 28) and was chosen to watch while Jesus prayed in the Garden of Gethsemane (Matt. xxvi. 37; Mark xiv. 33) certainly lends color to his earlier leadership, though we must not forget James and John. Peter's readiness to act as spokesman for the Twelve goes in the same direction, though this impulsiveness was probably temperamental and not by any authority on the part of the Twelve. When Jesus asked the opinion of the Twelve about His own personal claims Peter spoke in their behalf (Matt. xvi. 15 f.; Mark viii. 29; Luke ix. 20). But Peter spoke up just as quickly and rebuked Jesus for predicting His death. Even here Peter probably represented the sentiments of the Twelve who still expected a political kingdom not consonant with Christ's death. Mark gives a touch here that seems to make Jesus read approval of Peter's protest in the faces of the disciples: "But He, turning about, and seeing His disciples, rebuked Peter, and saith, Get thee behind Me, Satan; for thou mindest not the things of God, but the things of men" (Mark viii. 33). If the Twelve followed the lead of Peter when he asserted his determination to die for Christ though all others forsook him (Matt. xxvi. 35; Mark xiv. 31), we may recall also the fact that they likewise followed the lead of Judas Iscariot when he found fault with Mary of Bethany for wasting the money for the ointment (John xii. 4-6; Matt. xxvi. 8 f.; Mark xiv. 4 f.). In fact, but for John's later account, we should not know that Judas was the one who made the suggestion which met the approval of all the Twelve.

There is at any rate no proof that Peter was an official leader of the Twelve before the Resurrection of Jesus. Judas apparently held the position of Treasurer and carried the bag. He was not suspected of being a thief till later (John xii. 6) and seems to have had the confidence of all except Jesus, who knew his real nature all the time (John vi. 70 f.). So far as we know no other man held any office in the group. Jesus Himself was the Master, the Teacher, the Rabbi, the Lord (John xiii. 13). Peter by no means monopolized the activities of the Twelve. Jesus addresses a sequel to Philip (John vi. 5). Andrew volunteers a suggestion (John vi. 8). John reported his narrow zeal to Jesus (Luke ix. 49 f.). John and James suggest the calling down of fire from heaven on the Samaritan village (Luke ix. 51-6). Philip and Andrew come to Jesus with the problem of the Greeks (John xii. 22). In the last discourses we note inquiries from Peter (John xiii. 36), Thomas (xiv. 5), Philip (xiv. 8), Judas, the brother of James (xiv. 22). They all address Jesus a personal query, "Is it I?" after the dreadful disclosure by Jesus that one of them should betray Him (Matt. xxvi. 22; Mark xiv. 19). There was no lack of individual initiative because of Peter's aggressiveness or of Judas' official rank.

Indeed, the frequent contentions among the Twelve as to who was greatest among them seems to show clearly that there was no acknowledged or recognized leader among them other than Jesus. The official position of Judas may well have led him to feel that he was the natural one to stand next in authority to Jesus. The self-assumed spokesmanship of Peter would be resented by Judas as contesting his claims and aspirations. Peter would probably be scornful of a mere financier as the chief interpreter of the kingdom of heaven. Perhaps the other ten noticed the growing rivalry between Peter and Judas and were not without their own aspirations for the primacy in the political kingdom which they all expected as an inheritance from their Pharisaic environment. The first time that the dispute among the disciples is noted, it comes up in an academic form: "Who then is the greatest in the kingdom of heaven?" (Matt. xviii. 1). This question the disciples asked Jesus as if it were an abstract proposition, but they had first had "a reasoning among them, which of them should be greatest" (Luke ix. 46). "In the house" in Capernaum Jesus took up their academic query and probed this "reasoning of their heart" (Luke ix. 47) and asked them pointedly: "What were ye reasoning in the way?" (Mark ix. 34). "But they held their peace; for they had disputed one with another, who *was* the greatest" (Mark ix. 35). They were evidently ashamed for Jesus to know this skeleton of jealousy in the family closet. But Jesus sought to nip this sin in the bud. He sat down and took a little child (Peter's own child, tradition has it) and called the Twelve and set this child by His side in the midst of the disciples. Then Jesus gave the Twelve an object lesson in humility as the proof of real greatness and self-seeking as evidence of littleness. "Whosoever therefore shall humble himself as this little child, the same is the greatest in the kingdom of heaven" (Matt. xviii. 4). This incident seems to show conclusively that as yet no one is the acknowledged leader of the Twelve, for apparently they all aspire to that position and actually dispute over the proposition. It is now just a little over six months till Christ's death and after the summer of special teaching on the subject of the King and the kingdom.

But the case is worse than this. Just before reaching Jericho on the last journey to Jerusalem at the close of which comes the Cross "came to Him the mother of the sons of Zebedee with her sons" (Matt. xx. 20; cf. Mark x. 35). The people were now on tip-toe of expectation that the political Messianic kingdom was to be set up on Christ's arrival in Jerusalem (Luke xix. 11). No more time was to be lost if the long-continued dispute for the primacy among the Twelve was to be settled. James and John with Salome their mother concluded to take time by the forelock and risk all by a bold request for the two chief places for themselves: "Grant that we sit, one on Thy right hand, and one on Thy left hand, in Thy glory" (Mark x. 37), "in Thy kingdom" (Matt. xx. 21). It is the glory of the earthly Messianic kingdom, the consummation of which they believe is now at hand. They utterly misconceive the character of Christ's work, as He proceeds to show, but now at least there is outspoken opposition to the rival claims of Peter and Judas. If this assertiveness of James and John surprises one, it is to be noted that they stand by their position as candidates for the chief places even after Christ's mystical language and say, "We are able." "And when the ten heard it, they began to be moved with indignation concerning James and John" (Mark x. 41). Clearly there is no open leadership, but only rival claims moved by jealousy. The gravity of the matter is increased by the fact that this demand of James and John is made immediately after Jesus has spoken of His death.

But there is a sadder friction still. Peter and John were chosen by Christ to arrange the details for the observance of the Passover meal (Luke xxii. 8). So "when the hour was come, He sat down, and the apostles with Him" (Luke xxii. 14), but not before "there arose a contention among them which of them is accounted to be greatest" (Luke xxii. 24). The occasion for this fresh outbreak of jealousy was the order of precedence in reclining at the table. The post of honor was apparently the place right in front of Jesus. If so, though it is a disputed point, the honor fell to the Beloved Disciple (John xiii. 23 f.), not to Simon Peter. Swete (Mark *in loco*) argues that the apostles reclined in their usual order of precedence. But, if so, why the contention? In fact, did they have a usual order of precedence at table? I see no conclusive evidence of it. The orientals were very punctilious about table etiquette as in modern state or court functions. But the primacy among the Twelve seems the one point on which they could not agree. They show their pique and ambition at this very hour when the heart of Jesus is all aglow with emotion. Their conduct is so bad that Jesus tells them that they are acting like the heathen (Luke xxii. 25). They kept up their contention during the meal till Jesus arises from the table and gives them an object lesson in humility by offering to wash their feet (John xiii. 1-11).

It seems clear, therefore, that no one was the real leader of the Twelve as they face the death of Christ. It is doubtful if the official position of Judas ever gave him ranking place save in a perfunctory way, or if Peter was the acknowledged chief till the Pentecostal blessing. There is evidence that Jesus showed special concern for Peter in His prayer for him (Luke xxii. 31, περὶ σοῦ in contrast with ὑμᾶς), in the special message to Peter (Mark xvi. 7), and in the reinstatement and charge to feed Christ's sheep (John xxi. 15-19) as Christ had already foretold (Luke xxii. 32).

Dr. Wright thinks that Judas was titular leader at first, "for he held the bag, the symbol of authority," but had long been losing prestige, and that a coterie "wanted to take the bag from Judas and give it to Peter, that Peter might become the acknowledged leader, as he already was in practice." I doubt if the facts brought out above justify such a simple solution as that, since the general rivalry and open demand of James and John argue against any real leadership apart from Jesus. This conclusion of our study leaves us no nearer a decision regarding the meaning of ὁ εἷς in Mark xiv. 10 than we were at the beginning. The Greek idiom allows either "the first" or "the notorious one" of the Twelve. The facts in the Gospels do not give a clear decision. Wright says: "I press for this meaning [the first] of ὁ εἷς, believing it to be the simplest and best.'' But I fail to see how one is to reach a final conclusion without more light. Certainly, if Judas was ever the recognized leader, his fall was all the greater in the end.

CHAPTER IX

THE FOURTH GOSPEL IN THE LIGHT OF MODERN SCHOLARSHIP

The Fourth Gospel challenges interest from every point of view. It is a work of supreme art, some would say "the supreme literary work of the world." It has the dramatic quality of Shakespeare, the simplicity of Homer, the profundity of Job. There are only thirty pages of it, but it tells us more about Jesus than the Synoptic Gospels and all other books in the world. The vocabulary is limited and the Greek is very simple, though accurate, vernacular *Koiné*, while it breathes a Hebrew soul. It is the Holy of Holies of religious books, but it has not escaped criticism, as, indeed, it ought not to escape it. Modern men wish no fetish in their sacred books. They only ask that the canons of literary criticism be applied fairly to the Gospel of John as to Shakespeare and Homer. Certainly no one can claim that the acceptance of the Johannine authorship of the Fourth Gospel is due to obscurantism on the part of modern scholars. The fiercest controversy of New Testament criticism has raged around this book. The fight is not yet over, but continually takes on new aspects as it proceeds. Lightfoot says: "The genuineness of St. John's Gospel is the center of the position of those who uphold the historical truth of the record of our Lord Jesus Christ given us in the New Testament" (*Biblical Essays,* p. 47). Bacon agrees "with Bishop Lightfoot as to the vital character of the issues involved," while he rejects the implications in Lightfoot's statement (*The Fourth Gospel in Research and Debate,* p. 2).

It is interesting to note that two of the men who made the earliest formidable attacks on the Johannine authorship withdrew their criticisms after discussion. This was not true of Edward Evanson who in 1792 began the modern attack on the Fourth Gospel, but it was true of Bretschneider who in 1820 published in Latin a short, but powerful attack on the Johannine authorship. He put forth the thesis tentatively that the book was written in the middle of the second century by a presbyter of Alexandria. But after Lücke, Tholuck, Olshausen and others had answered his criticisms, he formally retracted his position and expressed his conviction of the genuineness of the book. Likewise Strauss repudiated all the Gospels as myths in his *Life of Jesus* in 1835. Under the strictures of Lücke, Neander, and De Witte he also withdrew his objections to the genuineness of John's Gospel, but he later took back this conviction. Baur boldly claimed that the Gospel of John was written between A. D. 160 and 170.

The battle waxed hot during the latter half of

the nineteenth century. But step by step the date was pushed back. Zeller and Scholten made it 150, but Hilgenfeld chose 130. Renan hit upon 100 and Harnack now puts it not later than 110. Those were doughty champions who took up the cudgels against the school of Baur, men like Lightfoot, Westcott, Ezra Abbot, Godet. To-day the conflict goes on. The Johannine authorship is denied by B. W. Bacon, C. F. Burney, Percy Gardner, A. E. Garvie, Grill, H. J. and O. Holtzmann, Harnack, Jülicher, Loisy, McGiffert, Moffatt, Pfleiderer, Reville, Schmiedel, E. F. Scott, Wernle, Wrede. This is a formidable list of recent scholars and shows that the fight is not over. But on the other hand one can name men like Marcus Dods, James Drummond, James Orr, Sanday, Stanton, Watkins, Zahn, who have struck powerful blows in behalf of the authenticity of this Gospel.

The external evidence is much stronger than it once was, partly because of fresh discoveries. The line of argument by which the date of the Fourth Gospel is approximately fixed is simple enough. Irenæus, Bishop of Lyons in Gaul, in his letter to Florinus (about A. D. 180) tells of his being a disciple of Polycarp, and of "the accounts which he gave of his intercourse with John and others who had seen the Lord." Polycarp was martyred A. D. 155, and was a Christian eighty-six years and a personal follower of John the Apostle. Polycarp was not simply alive when John wrote the Gospel, but was intimate with him, and in his

Epistle quotes the First Epistle of John. Now Irenæus quotes the Fourth Gospel a hundred times, credits the Gospel to the Apostle John, and accepts only the four Gospels which we know today as those according to Matthew, Mark, Luke, and John. Theophilus of Antioch (about A. D. 180) in his three books addressed to Autolycus, a heathen, quotes John by name as one of the Evangelists. So also Clement of Alexandria, head of the catechetical school there from A. D. 189 onward, quotes the four Gospels over four hundred times and cites John's Gospel by name. Tertullian of Carthage (about A. D. 200) quotes from almost every chapter of the Fourth Gospel and credits it to John the Apostle. But let us go back to Asia. The *Diatessaron* of Tatian is a blended harmony of the four Gospels and of these only. It begins with the first verse of the Fourth Gospel and closes with the Epilogue of this Gospel. The date cannot be later than A. D. 170, more probably A. D. 160. The discovery of the Armenian manuscript of Tatian's *Diatessaron* in 1880 led to great excitement among scholars of the world and soon (in 1888) an Arabic manuscript of the now famous book was found in Egypt. Since Tatian selected only our present four Gospels for his Harmony, it was at once clear that these Gospels had had general acceptation for a long time. Now Tatian was a disciple of Justin Martyr who in his Apologies and Dialogue with Trypho frequently quotes from the "Memoirs of the Apostles" what we find in our four Gospels. He quotes freely, but it seems probable that he refers to our four Gospels, and the *Diatessaron* of Tatian, his pupil, seems to make it certain. If so, the date of John's Gospel goes back to A.D. 130. Lightfoot and Zahn have proven the genuineness of the seven shorter (Vossian) Epistles of Ignatius (proven by the epistle of Polycarp to the Philippians). The date of these Epistles of Ignatius is A.D. 109-116. Zahn (*Introduction to New Testament*, III, 176) shows how unmistakable is the influence of the Gospel of John on these Ignatian Epistles: "This dependence of Ignatius upon John has been used as an argument against the genuineness of the Ignatian letters." We have thus come close to the time of John's own life, if he lived to the close of the first century, as he is generally believed to have done. There is much more confirmatory evidence in the use of the Fourth Gospel by Basilides in the first quarter of the second century, the use of it in the twentieth Clementine Homily, and by the Epistle to Diognetus. "All the discoveries of the past century proved to be favourable to the Johannine authorship of the book. No discovery has given aid to the opponents of that fact" (Hayes, *John and His Writings*, 1917, p. 129).

But did John live to this good old age? The testimony to this effect is almost unanimous. Irenæus expressly says: "John remained among them in Asia up to the time of Trajan" (*Adv. Haer.* ii. 22) and "John, the disciple of the Lord, who also lay on his breast, likewise published a Gospel while dwelling at Ephesus" (*Adv. Haer.* iii. 1). Trajan reigned A. D. 98-117. The Irenæus tradition is supported by Clement of Alexandria, Tertullian, Eusebius, Augustine, Jerome, and other great writers, to the effect that John the Apostle lived to a good old age in Ephesus and wrote the Fourth Gospel. And yet the early martyrdom of John is championed by great names to-day, by men like Bacon, Burkitt, Bousset, Jülicher, Loisy, Menzies, Moffatt, Pfleiderer, Schmiedel, Johannes Weiss. The testimony, it must be confessed, is more specious than convincing. We have the promise of martyrdom for James and John in the words of Jesus in Mark 10:39; Matt. 20:23. Both Origen and Jerome declared that the sufferings of John in exile in Patmos amply fulfilled the words of Jesus. The church calendars commemorate James and John as martyrs, probably because of the promise of Jesus. The only real historical evidence for the early death of John is what is called the "Papias tradition" as given by Georgius Hamartolus (George the Sinful) of the ninth century in his *Chronicle.* He says: "Papias, the Bishop of Hierapolis, having become an eyewitness of this one, declares in the second book of the Oracles of the Lord that John was put to death by the Jews, having evidently fulfilled with his brother the prediction of Christ concerning him, and his own confessions and assent in regard to this." This statement is appealed to in proof of the fact that John was killed at the same time as James in A. D. 44 (Cf. Acts 12:1 f.). But he does not say that. In truth, he expressly asserts in the same paragraph: "After Domitian, Nerva reigned one year; and he, having recalled John from the island, dismissed him to live in Ephesus." Nerva reigned A. D. 96-98. The only point claimed about John's death by George the Sinful is that John suffered martyrdom when an old man in Ephesus, not in Jerusalem in A. D. 44. There is nothing at all inconsistent with the Johannine authorship of the Fourth Gospel in this statement if it is true. But even this item will not stand examination. He appeals to Origen as saying in his commentary on Matthew that "John hath suffered martyrdom," intimating that he has learned this from the successors of the Apostles. But Hayes (*John and His Writings*, p. 132) shows that "when we consult the original we find that George has misunderstood and misinterpreted Origen, who says that John's exile to Patmos and his sufferings there were a sufficient martyrdom in themselves to fulfil the Lord's prophecy concerning the cup he should drink, and has no slightest intimation that John was killed by the Jews either at the same time with James or at any later date." We have only fragments of the works of Papias, but the quotation made by George the Sinful does not say that John was killed at the same time as James. There is also an epitome of the Chronicle of Philip (fifth century) called the de

Boor Fragment (seventh or eighth century) which says: "Papias in his second book says that John the Divine and James his brother were killed by the Jews." Moffatt (*Introduction to the Literature of the New Testament,* p. 604) accepts this as conclusive evidence that Papias asserted the death of John at the hands of the Jews, though he is unwilling to say that it was at the same time as that of James. But, if Papias did say that, it would not prove that John did not live to a good old age and so could have written the Gospel. Against it, however, is the tremendous positive evidence of many early writers who must have known what Papias said. Besides, if John was put to death early, who was the John at the Jerusalem Conference mentioned in Galatians, 2:9? Schwartz (*Tod der Söhne Zebedai,* 1904) argues strongly for A. D. 44 as the date of John's death and Wellhausen (on Mark 19:39) agreed that he had proven his point. But, as we have seen, the critics have here grasped at shadows to prove a case.

There is yet another turn in the wheel. Papias, whose testimony is so doubtful about the death of John, is again appealed to. This time Eusebius (*Hist. Eccl.* iii. 39) gives the quotation: "If, then, anyone came who had been a follower of the elders, I questioned him in regard to the words of the elders—what Andrew or what Peter said, or what was said by Philip, or by Thomas, or by James, or by John, or by Matthew, or by any other of the disciples of the Lord, and what things Aristion and the presbyter John, the disciples of the Lord, say." Eusebius understood Papias to speak of two Johns, the Apostle John and the Presbyter John, and said so. A number of modern scholars agree with the interpretation of Eusebius and credit the Fourth Gospel to this imaginary Presbyter John. Bacon, Dobschütz, Harnack, McGiffert, Moffatt, take him to be the author. Dom Chapman's book, *John the Presbyter and the Fourth Gospel* (1911), proves, as nearly as can be proved, that there was no such man. Papias does not say that he is other than the Apostle John. He calls all the Apostles, please note, "elders" (presbyters). Peter calls himself presbyter or elder (1 Peter 5:1) as the author of II and III John does. Besides, Papias makes a contrast (Hayes, *op. cit.*, p. 139), not between two persons, but between two methods of reporting, "one by report of what John the Apostle had said, and one by hearing the Apostle himself." This is obvious on close attention. We come back to Irenæus, Polycarp, and the Apostle John. Only Polycarp stands between Irenæus and John. Irenæus says: "Then John, the disciple of the Lord, who also had leaned upon his breast, did himself publish a Gospel during his residence at Ephesus in Asia" (*Ad. Haer.* III 1). Modern research not simply has not overturned this specific statement of one who knew Polycarp, John's own disciple, but has confirmed and strengthened it.

Discussion will go on as it has done in the past. Delff (*Das Vierte Evangelium wiedergestellt,* 1890; *Neue Beiträge zur Kritik und Erklärung des vierten Evangeliums,* 1890) has advanced an interesting hypothesis. He admits that the Fourth Gospel was written by the one described in the book as "the disciple whom Jesus loved." This is, in fact, the claim of the book itself (John 21: 20-24). Irenæus refers to John as the one who leaned on Jesus' breast at the Supper. Delff argues ingeniously and skilfully that this disciple lived in Jerusalem (John 19: 27), was an acquaintance of the high priest (18:15 f.), was on intimate terms with Jesus and the disciples, though not one of the twelve apostles. Even Sanday (*The Criticism of the Fourth Gospel,* 1905, pp. 98 ff.) is attracted by the hypothesis, though he still holds to the Johannine authorship as more probable. There are, however, some patent difficulties in the way of this position. For one thing, one has to suppose a "supernumerary apostle" (Sanday), who was on even more intimate terms with Jesus than the inner circle (Peter, James, and John) of the Synoptic Gospels, and yet he is not mentioned by them at all. This is, of course, possible, but highly improbable. And then this unknown intimate friend of Jesus is a companion of Simon Peter just as we see them in the early chapters of Acts. Once more, this "beloved disciple," if not John, has a special dislike for him, because his name is not mentioned in the book. Besides, the brother of John, James, is likewise passed by without specific naming. Once only "the sons of Zebedee" (John 21:2) are listed with the seven. If John is the author of this Gospel, we can see why he would not refer to himself by name and also why he would omit the name of his own brother James. So Luke has no mention of his own name in Acts, or of Titus, who was possibly his brother. In the "we sections" he has only "we" and "us." It is possible to combine this theory of Delff with the "Presbyter John" hypothesis, but there is no real gain in the suggestion of Delff. It bristles with difficulties of its own. Swete has a note in the July (1916) *Journal of Theological Studies* on *"The Disciples Whom Jesus Loved"* in which he suggests the Rich Young Ruler as the "Beloved Disciple," but this is pure hypothesis. Others have suggested John Mark. But the Irenæus tradition, to follow Moffatt's phrase, stands still in our path. "The first known commentary on any New Testament book was a commentary on the Fourth Gospel written by Heracleon, A. D. 145" (Hayes, *op. cit.*, p. 148).

Others have attacked the unity and integrity of the Fourth Gospel, but with little success. The book hangs together in a wonderful way. Wendt (*The Gospel According to John: An Inquiry into its Genesis and Historical Value*, 1892 has proposed an apostolic kernel as the original nucleus left by John which was enlarged by a redactor or redactors. The same view is presented by Briggs

(*General Introduction to the Study of Holy Scripture,* 1899). But the book is too much of a piece and the same linguistic and theological characteristics pervade the whole. There is a Prologue (1:1-18) which is a real introduction to the whole line of thought. There is no reason to regard the Prologue as a philosophical addition to the book (Harnack, *Ueber das Verhältniss des Prologs des vierten Evangeliums zum ganzen Werke,* 1892). The Epilogue (chapter 21) is by the same hand, though it may have been added later, as the book seems to end at 20:31.

The relation of the Fourth Gospel to the Apocalypse has caused special trouble because of the linguistic features of the Apocalypse. Beyond a doubt there is room for this criticism as anyone familiar with Greek can see. There are lapses in case and number, loose and free handling of infinitives and participles, less care for the regular idioms of written speech. One sees the same phenomena now and then in other parts of the New Testament, particularly in the impassioned passages of Paul's Epistles, and in the ancient Greek writers. These solecisms are especially common in the more illiterate papyri of the *Koiné.* Various theories have been suggested to explain the situation. One is difference of authorship. Either John wrote the Apocalypse and not the Gospel, or *vice versa.* A John is claimed by the book as the writer of the Apocalypse (Rev. 1:9). Moffatt (*Introduction to the Literature of the*

New Testament, p. 615) credits the Apocalypse to the Presbyter John, and the Gospel he considers of unknown authorship (*ibid.*, p. 570). Moulton (*Prolegomena*, p. 9) suggests that, if the Apocalypse is Johannine and as late as A. D. 95, either the Gospel was by another author or was revised by the author of John 21:24. This latter suggestion is quite possible. John and Peter were regarded by the Sanhedrin as "unlearned and ignorant men" (Acts 4:13) and it is precisely the Apocalypse and II Peter that have more linguistic idiosyncrasies (Cf. Robertson, *Grammar of the Greek New Testament in the Light of Historical Research*, pp. 134 ff.).

But our troubles with the critics are by no means over if the Johannine authorship is conceded as it should be. The balance of evidence is distinctly on that side and far outweighs the testimony for Plato's works or for those of Thucydides. James Drummond, himself a Unitarian and free from suspicion of prejudice in favor of the Johannine authorship, has written a powerful defense of the book, *The Character and Authorship of the Fourth Gospel*, 1904. He says (p. 514): "In literary questions we cannot look for demonstration, and where opinion is so much divided we must feel some uncertainty in our conclusions; but on weighing the arguments for and against to the best of my power, I must give my own judgment in favor of the Johannine authorship." This is the cautious decision of a scholar who has long considered the whole problem. But it is objected that even so the book has the bias of a theological pamphlet and is devoid of historical value or objectivity. It is the subjective theorizing of a man who is anxious to make out a case, to prove the divinity of Jesus Christ (John 20:30 f.). "The narrative is composed with the set intention of proving that Jesus is the Christ, the Son of God" (Scott, *The Fourth Gospel: Its Purpose and Theology*, 1906, pp. 1 f.). But does this fact vitiate it as a veracious interpretation of Christ? The Gospel according to Matthew is also written with the set purpose of proving that Jesus of Nazareth is the Messiah of Jewish hope and promise. Every history worth reading has a philosophy of interpretation, else it is a mere chronicle of details. Bacon (*The Fourth Gospel in Research and Debate*, p. 12) makes a more serious charge: "Divine intention and operation are not interpreted by historical fact, but historical fact by divine intention and operation. What an incarnation of deity must say and do in order to make clear the redemptive plan, this is what is said and done. The selection of seven 'signs' is avowedly made for the purpose of producing faith in this sense." One is bound to reply that Bacon has misunderstood the author's statement of his purpose in 20:30 f. He does say that he wrote to create faith in Jesus, but not by the perversion of the facts. He has selected a few salient and pertinent "signs" out of many others like them that show the truth of his thesis. This is the way of all real historians and biographers and it is the only way to deal with a mass of details.

It is charged that a philosophical theory colors the writer's story. His Logos doctrine is said to make Jesus a wholly unreal being and to be a mere imitation of the Stoics and Philo. Scott (*op. cit.*, p. 173) says: "There can be little doubt that by thus importing the doctrines of the Logos into the Gospel record, John is not only compelled to do violence to historical fact, but empties the life of Christ of much of its real worth and grandeur while seeming to enhance it." He has much to the same effect: "The doctrine of the Logos, born of philosophical theory, has nothing to do with the historical revelations in Jesus, and is wholly inadequate to explain it" (p. 175). Certainly the Stoics made much of the Logos as the Reason of the Universe, as Plato had done, and Heraclitus before him. Philo was fond of the term and carried it over into his interpretation of Judaism. The term lay ready to hand for John if he cared to use it to expound the eternal and cosmic relations of Jesus Christ. He did not use it as a full and complete presentation of all aspects of Christ's nature and life any more than this is true of terms like the Son of God, the Son of Man, the Messiah, the Light of the World, the Life, the Truth, the Way. But it is by no means clear that John got the word from the Stoics or from Philo. The Jews used *Memra* (Word) in a personified sense in the

Targums, and Wisdom is personified in Proverbs. Indeed, J. Rendel Harris (*The Expositor*, August to December, 1916) shows that all the distinctive phraseology in John's Prologue could have come from Proverbs 8. But John is to be commended, not condemned, for his effort to interpret Christ to the men of culture of his day.

A further objection is that the author has invented the conversations and attributed the language to Jesus for dramatic effect as Thucydides composed the Funeral Oration of Pericles. The same general style pervades the narrative portions of the Gospel and the dialogues. That is true, and beyond a doubt the words of Jesus have blended in places with the reminiscences of the author. It is, however, a pertinent question whether the style of John has not to a large extent been influenced by the mood of Jesus here seen? We have this same "Johannine" type of teaching in Luke 10:21-24; Matt. 11:25-29. This *logion*, apparently also in Q, has to be accounted for. One is reminded of the report of Socrates by Xenophon and Plato. A good discussion of this aspect of the subject is found in Askwith's *Historical Value of the Fourth Gospel* (1910) and Watson's *Mysticism of St. John's Gospel* (1916).

Once more the Fourth Gospel is discredited in comparison with the Synoptic Gospels. They are held up as objective history while the Fourth Gospel is treated as pure invention with a totally different picture of Jesus. "Which of them represents the real Jesus, is for historical criticism to determine; and the heart of the problem is the Gospel attributed to John, with its reversal of the Synoptic conception. Both conceptions cannot represent the apostolic story" (Bacon, *op. cit.*, p. 13). That puts the criticism in a nutshell. Perhaps the best answer to Bacon is to quote Moffatt, who also, with Bacon, rejects the Johannine authorship (*op. cit.*, p. 540): "The day is now over, or almost over, when the Fourth Gospel and the Synoptists could be played off against each other in a series of rigid antitheses, as though the one were a matter-of-fact and homogeneous chronicle, and the other a spiritual reading of the earlier tradition. The problem is too delicate and complex for such crude methods. Recent criticism of the Synoptic Gospels has brought them nearer to the Fourth Gospel." This is obviously true. It is no "Jesus or Christ" controversy. In each of the Four Gospels Jesus is Son of God and Son of Man. The same great lines are in each picture and Paul follows suit. The shading is different, but the portrait is the same.

The discussion will go on through the years. Men will take this view or that, but no one can be indifferent to this most wonderful of all books. "I believe the writings of John have been blotted by more penitents' tears and have won more hearts for the Redeemer than all the rest put together" (Culross, *John Whom Jesus Loved*, p. 212). "Others may have been dominant in the past. Others may rule in the present. The future belongs to John. He increasingly will come to his own" (Hayes, *op. cit.*, p. 12). John has a bold and a clear message for men of culture who have doubts because of philosophy or science. He lays all knowledge and all truth at the feet of Jesus and calls upon all thoughtful men to do the same.

Shortly before his death Dr. William Sanday wondered if after all he had not been too positive in his position concerning the Fourth Gospel. In "Divine Overruling," p. 61, he says: "I'm afraid there is one important point on which I was probably wrong—the Fourth Gospel." Dr. Sanday was always candid and open to fresh evidence while at heart loyal to the truth as he saw it. He first won great fame by his luminous and able treatise in 1872 entitled "The Authorship and Historical Character of the Fourth Gospel Considered in Reference to the Contents of the Gospel itself." In this volume Dr. Sanday revealed the clear insight, the cautious temper, the comprehensive grasp that marked all his later productions. With fine poise he urged that "it is useless to point to the culture of the Greek, when beneath it there lies the indisputable stamp and character of the Jew" (p. 303). He concludes (p. 304): "The Gospel is the work of the Apostle, the son of Zebedee; it is the record of an eye witness of the life of our Lord Jesus Christ; and its historical character is such as under the circumstances might be expected—it needs no adventitious commendation to make it higher." That was the verdict of the brilliant young scholar of Oxford whose star was already rising while the Cambridge trio (Hort, Lightfoot, Westcott) were in their glory. Dr. Sanday once told me that he considered Hort the ablest of the three. But Sanday was not necessarily bound to an opinion because he had previously advocated it. In 1905 Dr. Sanday (*The Criticism of the Fourth Gospel*) returns again to the problem of the Fourth Gospel and reviews with great care and fairness the vigorous controversy of the generation before. He reviews the work of able defenders of the Johannine authorship like Zahn, B. Weiss, Luthardt, Ezra Abbot, Watkins, Lightfoot, Westcott, Drummond and that of those who reject it like Wendt, Bacon, H. J. Holtzmann, Jülicher, Schmiedel, Wrede, Wernle, Loisy, Moffatt, McGiffert. Dr. Sanday in 1905 still holds to the unity of the Fourth Gospel and the probable Johannine authorship, though with nothing like the clearness and vigor shown in 1872. He is attracted by the view of Delff, Harnack, Schuerer, and Dobschutz that the Gospel was the work of the Beloved Disciple who may have been the so-called Presbyter John, or some other disciple in Jerusalem, though Sanday sees difficulties in the way of that view and hopes that on the whole John the Apostle is the author in spite of the difficulties in the way. But Sanday's temper is seen in these words (p. 157): "I do not honestly believe that everything happened as it is, or seems to be reported. But in saying this I must add that I also do not believe that, even if the argument were made good to the full extent alleged, it would at all decisively impugn the conclusion at which we have hitherto seemed to arrive—that the Gospel is really the work of an eyewitness and of St. John." So in Sanday we see the conflict of two generations reflected as in a mirror.

Some critics were beginning to look upon Johannine criticism as having settled the problem of the Fourth Gospel against the Apostle John. They were willing to admit a Johannine school or a disciple of John, but not the Apostle John as the real author. Charles is impressed by the resemblances in language and thought between the Fourth Gospel and the Apocalypse which "point decidedly to some connection between the two authors. The Evangelist was apparently at one time a disciple of the Seer, or they were members of the same religious circle in Ephesus" (*Revelation of St. John*, Vol. I, p. xxxiii). Every scholar has noticed the smoothness of the language in the Gospel and the grammatical uncouthness of the Apocalypse, but the underlying likeness is also there, whatever the explanation.

For myself I have never been able to see the utter incompatibility of the same author for both books, provided difference in circumstances was allowed. If we dismiss the hypothesis of a separate John the Presbyter and make the Apostle and Presbyter John the son of Zebedee as Dom Chapman so ably argues (*John the Presbyter and the Fourth Gospel,* 1911), then it is hard to resist the conclusion that the John of the Apocalypse is the Beloved Disciple of the Fourth Gospel (Sanday, *The Criticism of the Fourth Gospel,* p. 252). There is, to be sure, the dispute whether John was put to death by the Jews on the misinterpretation of Origen by George the Sinful (Hayes, *John and His Writings,* p. 132).

But scholars with lingering doubts on one side or the other of the age-long controversy have taken fresh interest in the book of Dr. C. F. Burney, Oriel Professor of the Interpretation of Holy Scripture at Oxford: (*The Aramaic Origin of the Fourth Gospel,* 1922). Critics had been emphasizing the Hellenistic character of the Fourth Gospel (chiefly the Logos in the Prologue) and had overlooked the Semitic character of the language. "There are few Hebraisms in detail." "In the formal grammar the Greek is much like the vernacular (and literary) κοινή, but the cast of thought is wholly Hebrew." So I had written in my "Grammar of the Greek New Testament in the Light of Historical Research," p. 133. There is a Semitic flavor in the Fourth Gospel that the Greek dress did not hide. The possibility that in the Apocalypse we have John's real style of uncouth Greek while in the Gospel his work has had revision, had attracted me (*Ibid,* p. 137). John and Peter are termed ἀγράμματοι καὶ ἰδιῶται by the Sanhedrin in Acts 4:13. There is a slight hint at revision of the Gospel in John 21:24 in the use of οἴδαμεν by those who endorse the Beloved Disciple as the author of the book in contrast to οἶμαι in verse 25. But this view has been regarded as a rather desperate resort for those who are determined to cling to the Johannine authorship of the Fourth Gospel.

Lightfoot had already urged that the Fourth Gospel revealed distinct traces of Aramaic influence (*Biblical Essays,* 1893, pp. 126-144). The Greek is not ungrammatical Greek, but it is cast in a Hebrew mould. It is what no native Greek could have written" (p. 135). Dr. Burney laments that the point of Lightfoot was not taken up by New Testament scholars (p. 1). Other men had long ago suggested that the Fourth Gospel had an Aramaic original, but detailed proof was not forthcoming. Schlatter in 1902 (*Die Sprache und Heimat des vierten Evangelisten*) had demonstrated the Semitic character of the Fourth Gospel by citing Rabbinic parallels to the language of much of it (verse by verse). The trouble is that few New Testament scholars are experts in the Semitic languages. So Dr. Burney comes to the study of the Fourth Gospel from the Semitic side. This fact will be counted against him. Dr. James Moffatt is not impressed by the arguments for minimizing the Alexandrian influences in the Gospel, but thinks that Dr. Burney's book will call attention to the Fourth Gospel along new lines (*The Hibbert Journal,* July, 1922, p. 783).

But Rev. L. W. Grensted is greatly impressed by Dr. Burney's stimulating suggestion (*New Light on the Fourth Gospel, The Interpreter*, July, 1922, pp. 263-9). He notes that since the time of Erasmus the Hellenists have had it all their own way with the New Testament, but that now "all serious New Testament scholars must in the future know Hebrew and Aramaic, or, at least, walk humbly when the Semitist speaks" (p. 269). The New Testament as we have it is Greek, the current *κοινή* of the first century A.D., as the papyri prove. But it is impossible to cut the New Testament entirely free from its Semitic environment. We know that Jesus spoke Aramaic to the usual Jewish people, but probably Greek on occasion when in Greek speaking communities. Mark translates some of the Aramaic sayings of Jesus into Greek. Papias states that Matthew wrote the Logia of Jesus in Hebrew (Aramaic) which each one translated as he was able. It is now maintained by many scholars that this was the Q of criticism, the non-Markan source common to our Greek Matthew and to Luke. Some scholars argue that Mark was first written in Aramaic. Translation from the Aramaic sources, therefore, undoubtedly played a considerable part in the preparation of our Gospels. Luke was probably a Greek, but in the Gospel 1:5 to 2:52 he clearly made use of Aramaic sources either oral or written or both, with many earmarks of the Semitic original in sharp contrast with the literary introduction in 1:1-4. In the rest of the Gospel Luke has Semitic touches due either to the use of the Septuagint or to the Semitic material used by him. That is true also in the opening chapters of the Acts without accepting the view of Prof. C. C. Torrey that all of Acts 1-15 is a translation from an Aramaic original. We now know that what Dr. James Hope Moulton called "Translation-Greek" is a much larger factor in the New Testament than he admitted. It is still clear that the New Testament was written in the current Greek of the first century A. D., chiefly in the vernacular, but with some distinctly literary portions. But it must not be forgotten that Jesus lived in Palestine and read the Hebrew Old Testament and spoke the Aramaic as well as the κοινή. The people of Palestine spoke Aramaic and some of them used the Greek also. But the background of Christianity is Semitic, not Greek. Palestine was a Semitic patch in the Græco-Roman world. The language of the New Testament is good κοινή, but the authors of the Gospels and the Acts necessarily worked on Semitic materials. It is less so of Paul who, though a Jew, wrote his Epistles freely without the use of sources save the quotations from the Old Testament (usually the Septuagint, though sometimes his own translation of the Hebrew). Charles has proven up to the hilt the Semitic character of the Apocalypse in conception and to a considerable extent in language. It is not necessary to go to the extreme that

Charles does and to make the Greek and grammar of the Apocalypse unlike anything in the world to see that it is Semitic in conception and style.

But Dr. Burney argues that in the Fourth Gospel the problem concerns Aramaisms, not Hebraisms. He thinks that the argument for the Aramaic original of the Fourth Gospel is much stronger than that for Mark's Gospel. Mark was Peter's "interpreter" and knew both Aramaic and Greek well and may only preserve Aramaic touches in his Greek. The chief Aramaisms claimed by Dr. Burney may be given in broad outline. It is not practicable here to discuss the details given by Dr. Burney, some of which are much more striking than others. But the broad lines of his argument may be given. He urges (p. 49) that "it is highly characteristic of Aramaic to open its sentences abruptly without the use of a connecting particle," whereas asyndeton is uncommon in Hebrew and Greek. The Synoptic writers use asyndeton rarely; it is common in the Fourth Gospel. Parataxis (p. 56) is common to both Hebrew and Aramaic, but the Fourth Gospel far surpasses the Synoptic books. "Sentences are regularly coördinated and linked by *καί*. Subordinate sentences are few and far between." The rarity of the genitive absolute in comparison with the Synoptic Gospels is noteworthy. Both Hebrew and Aramaic (p. 63) make frequent use of the *casus pendens*, much more common in John than in the Synoptic Gospels. This is not a very strong argument as the form of anacoluthon is common in the vernacular of all languages. John makes infrequent use of καί in comparison with the Synoptists (p. 66) partly because of asyndeton and partly because of the excessive use of οὖν (200 times in John, 57 in Matthew, 6 in Mark, 31 in Luke). One of the most striking points made by Dr. Burney is the suggestion (p. 70) that the Aramaic *dĕ* which has so many shades of meaning (that, who, which, when, in order that, inasmuch as, because) may lie behind the varied use of ἵνα in the Fourth Gospel and even of ὅτι (p. 76). He argues also (p. 87) that the historic present, so common in Mark (151 examples) and in John (164 examples, against 78 in Matthew partly same as in Mark, 4 or 6 in Luke) is due to the Aramaic idiom rather than to mere colloquial vivacity in Mark and John. Dr. Burney considers the most weighty form of evidence (p. 101) to be cases where the Aramaic and the Hebrew had different meanings or where the Aramaic was original. In John 7:38 he holds that in the unvocalized text the Aramaic word for "fountain" and for "belly" would be identical. He suggests "fountain" as correct. He points to Matt. 23:26 where καθάρισον corresponds to δότε ἐλεη μοσύνην in Luke 11:41. In Matthew we should have "Cleanse first what is within the cup" and in Luke "Cleanse what is within" (the cup) rather than "Give as alms what is within" (a very puzzling passage).

It is too soon to pass final judgment on the

problem raised by Dr. Burney. But his solution at least challenges consideration. If he is right and the Fourth Gospel itself is early in its Aramaic form, we see an answer to the enigma connected with the famous Johannine passage in the Logia of Jesus (Q) that has so long puzzled critics (Matt. 11:25-30 = Luke 10:21-22). The use of the "Son" and the "Father" in the earliest known document behind our Gospels is precisely of a piece with that in the Fourth and last of the Gospels. The genuineness of this type of teaching by Christ is greatly strengthened.

Once more, if the original of the Fourth Gospel was early (say by 75 A.D.) and by an eye-witness from Palestine, the book gains historical credibility as Westcott so ably argued. In that case Sanday in 1872 was nearer right than Sanday in 1905. And then the early date of the Synoptic Gospels receives fresh confirmation since the Fourth assumes their narrative.

It follows also that the difference in language between the Fourth Gospel and the Apocalypse vanishes. "Thus it appears that the case against identity of authorship of the Gospel and the Apocalypse can certainly not be maintained on the ground of date. The evidence is all in the other direction." (Burney, p. 152). This is Dr. Burney's conclusion after giving a "rough list of Semitisms common to the Fourth Gospel and the Apocalypse" (p. 150).

Dr. Burney is aware of the audacity of his

theory: "If the theory is soundly based, it must surely affect something like a revolution in current Johannine criticism" (p. 126). The testing of time will tell how much of truth lies in this prophecy.

Dr. Burney holds to the unity of the Fourth Gospel and the identity of authorship with the Apocalypse. He believes, however, that the John of the Apocalypse is the so-called Presbyter John of Papias and the Presbyter (the Elder) of the Johannine Epistles. Dr. Burney suggests (p. 149) that the Epistles were dictated to an amanuensis, who may have been the translator of the Gospel from Aramaic, as an explanation of the freedom from the solecisms of the Apocalypse.

Dr. Burney presents no new arguments against the Johannine authorship of the Fourth Gospel except that it is unlikely that the unschooled fisherman of Galilee should show so much rabbinical knowledge as Schlatter has shown. But if the Aramaic Gospel was written about A. D. 75, that is forty years after A. D. 35, the probable time of the remark recorded in Acts 4:13. The great knowledge of the Old Testament as shown in the Apocalypse is not inconsistent with full knowledge of the oral teaching of rabbis. Besides, much of this familiarity may be due to the teaching of Jesus. There is nothing whatever in the theory of Dr. Burney that rules out the Apostle John as the author of the Johannine books.

Dr. Burney argues that the Logos Doctrine in

the Prologue of the Fourth Gospel may well be suggested by the language of the Targums, as is so ably shown by Dr. J. Rendel Harris, rather than directly from Philo. In that case the Hellenism of the Fourth Gospel disappears. It is quite worth while to ask if after all the strained effort to find Greek influence in the New Testament teaching does not sometimes blind one to the tremendous influence of the Hebrew Scriptures, the very breath of these writers. Paul and Luke and the author of the Epistle to the Hebrews were certainly open to the influences of the Græco-Roman world, but not to the obscuring of Christ and of Christianity.

Synoptic criticism has shown the early date of Q and of Mark. Ramsay and Harnack have vindicated the historical value of Luke the author of the Gospel and the Acts, a veritable "Revolution in New Testament Criticism" as Dr. James Stalker has termed it. Would it not be the climax of this whole process if the Fourth Gospel should be shown to be early in its Aramaic original, to be Palestinian and Jewish and not Greek in thought and style, even in the end to be the work of John the Apostle? Stranger things have happened.

Principal Garvie's able volume, *The Beloved Disciple* (1922), argues that our present Fourth Gospel is the work of three men. The first is the Witness (W) of the life and teachings of Jesus. The second is the Evangelist (E), a disciple of the Witness. The Evangelist reproduces the reminiscences of the Witness with additions of his own like the Prologue and various other items. The third is the Redactor (R) who added the Appendix (chapter 21) with various comments here and there. Dr. Garvie makes a specious and plausible presentation, but one that leaves one unconvinced. The claims that he establishes a degree of historicity for the testimony of the Witness, but the same cannot be said for the Evangelist and the Redactor. So Dr. Garvie sets aside the comments of the Evangelist and of the Redactor when he is disposed to do so. The method of deciding between the work of each of these three writers is subjective and inclusive. In particular, the Evangelist is accused of exaggerating the supernaturalness of Jesus (p. 197).

We may be sure that the last word has not been said about the Fourth Gospel. Every man sees what he sees or thinks that he sees. For myself I welcome all research in this great and difficult field and my conviction still holds that the Johannine authorship solves more of the problems than any other one that has been presented.

It is not necessary to give a list of the recent books on the Fourth Gospel. The following books illustrate well enough the interest in various phases of the Johannine Problem: Wellhausen's *Das Evangelium Johannis* (1908), E. F. Scott's *The Historical and Religious Value of the Fourth Gospel* (1909), Spitta's *Das Johannesevangelium als Quelle der Geschichte Jesu* (1909), Worsley's

The Fourth Gospel and the Synoptics (1909), Askwith's *The Historical Value of the Fourth Gospel* (1910), Chapman's *John the Presbyter and the Fourth Gospel* (1911), Lewis's *Disarrangements in Fourth Gospel* (1911), Gardner's *The Ephesian Gospel* (1915), Watson's *Mysticism of St. John's Gospel* (1916), Robertson's *Divinity of Christ in the Gospel of John* (1916), Hayes's *John and His Writings* (1917), Harris's *Origin of the Prologue to St. John's Gospel* (1917), Strachan's *The Fourth Gospel: Its Significance and Environment* (1917), Jackson's *The Problem of the Fourth Gospel* (1918), Scott-Holland's *The Philosophy of Faith and the Fourth Gospel* (1919), Stanton's *Fourth Gospel* (1921), Loisy's *La Quatrième évangile* (2nd ed., 1921), Keisker's *Inner Witness of the Fourth Gospel* (1922), Burney's *Aramaic Origin of the Fourth Gospel* (1922), Garvie's *Beloved Disciple* (1922), Scott-Holland's *The Fourth Gospel* (1923).

Chapter X

MARK'S GOSPEL AND MODERN KNOWLEDGE

The Gospel of Mark confronts all modern discussion of the sources of our knowledge of Jesus. "No man can pretend to have seriously examined the historical basis of the Christian faith who has not to some extent applied the ordinary processes of historical criticism to the gospel of Mark" (Bacon, *The Beginnings of Gospel Story,* 1909, p. vii). That is a true statement of the case.

I. The Rights of Gospel Criticism: We agree at once with Miller when he says: "The gospels, like other documents of the past, must be examined according to strict historical methods" (*Our Knowledge of Christ,* 1914, p. 47). Only we insist that the investigation must be complete and include all the facts, and be free from prejudice against the contents of the gospels, and with a mind open to the explanation most in harmony with the facts. We can follow O. Holtzmann when he says: "Historical science is under an imperative obligation to furnish a picture of Jesus which shall be as far as possible trustworthy" (*Life of Jesus,* 1904, p. 1). The modern Christian wishes to know the full truth about the gospels. He desires to follow no "Mother Goose" legends as the basis of his knowledge of Jesus. Nothing is gained by obscurantism and credulity any more than by obdurate skepticism. It is true that "for the intelligent layman the problems raised by Biblical criticism become most acute when they concern the gospels and the life of Christ" (Miller, *Our Knowledge of Christ*, p. 48). But no intelligent minister or layman wishes to hide his head in the sand and refuse to see the facts. A good tonic for one who desires to see the worst that has been or can be said against the historical worth of our gospels, with an adequate reply, may be found in Thorburn's masterly volume, *The Mythical Interpretation of the Gospels* (1916). There is need, however, of the caveat that we do not put critical infallibility in the place of theological infallibility. The historical or scientific method of gospel criticism is the true one, but it is not axiomatic and not always certain. It is possible to develop and apply certain broad principles of study,[1] if only we avoid the intolerant dogmatism of a too narrow specialization. It is sufficient on this point to let Schweitzer speak. He is a bold and independent critic with his own pet theory of eschatology as the crux of Christ's teaching. Schweitzer is keen in his exposure of the narrowness of much criticism:

"Modern historical theology, therefore, with its three-quarters skepticism, is left at last with only

[1] See Burton, *Principles of Literary Criticism and the Synoptic Problem*, 1904.

a torn and tattered gospel of Mark in its hands" (*The Quest of the Historical Jesus,* 1910, p. 307).

He quotes (p. 331) Wrede as saying "that each critic retains whatever portion of the traditional sayings can be fitted into his construction of the facts and his conception of historical possibility and rejects the rest." In a word, Schweitzer adds:

"Only the catchwords with which the narrative is enlivened have been changed, being now taken in part from Nietzsche. The liberal Jesus has given place to the Germanic Jesus. This is a figure which has as little to do with the Marcan hypothesis as the 'liberal' Jesus had which preceded it" (p. 307).

Schweitzer thus wrote in 1909 of "the Germanic Jesus" as having supplanted both the "liberal" Jesus and the Jesus of Mark's gospel. Criticism has its undoubted rights and is a necessary tool in modern research; but, after all, it is only a tool, and the outcome depends upon the use made of the tool.

"In order to find in Mark the life of Jesus of which it is in search, modern theology is obliged to read between the lines a whole host of things, and those often the most important, and then to foist them upon the text by means of psychological conjecture" (Schweitzer, *ibid.,* p. 330).

II. The Synoptic Gospels and the Fourth Gospel: Criticism is unanimous in finding a wide difference in the character of the Synoptics and of the Fourth Gospel, whatever view is held about the authorship of the Gospel according to John. This difference of style is applied to the question of the deity of Jesus Christ in a ruthless fashion by Bacon: "On this question we are driven unavoidably to the alternative: either Synoptics or John" (*The Fourth Gospel in Research and Debate,* 1910, p. 4). He adds: "Both views can not be true, and to a very large extent it is the science of literary and historical criticism which must decide between them." But this extreme view can not be sustained, for, there are two passages in Mark's gospel (8:38; 13:32) where "the Father" and "the Son" are related as in John's Gospel. In one of these we have the antithesis, "neither the Son, but the Father" (13:32).

"It is, however, of real importance, in estimating the testimony of the two correlative forms 'the Father' and 'the Son' that one of the leading passages in St. Mark should bear this stamp" (Sanday, "The Deity of Christ in the Gospels," in his volume, *The Life of Christ in Recent Research,* 1907, p. 131).

It is true, however, that the historical worth of the Fourth Gospel is a separate problem from the Synoptic problem. The point to be emphasized here is that we must not stress the difference beyond the facts. There is a good discussion of the matter by Worsley in *The Fourth Gospel and the Synoptists* (1909). Gilbert finds in the Greek element of the Gospel of John "the capstone of the evidence that in this remarkable writing we have, not history and not biography, but a profound philosophical meditation in which the facts of the life of Jesus are treated with sovereign freedom" (*Jesus,* 1912, p. 71). This seems to me far too sweeping a statement of the facts about John's Gospel, but those of that temper may turn with interest to the Synoptic Gospels as more objective and more historical. It must be said, however, that those who come to the study of the Synoptic Gospels with fixed prejudices against the deity of Christ Jesus and the miraculous or the supernatural will find distinct difficulty also in these gospels.

"I would urge their consideration upon the attention of those in whose thoughts the question of the character of the Fourth Gospel overshadows all other gospel problems, and who, perhaps not unnaturally, are becoming somewhat weary of the discussion of the synoptic question" (Stanton, *The Gospels as Historical Documents,* Part II, 1909, p. 2).

Sanday insists that the gospels are histories and that "the Evangelists are not copyists but historians," while "yet the gospels are not exactly histories" (in *Oxford Studies in the Synoptic Problem,* 1911, pp. 12, 14). "The present state of the synoptic problem" (cf. H. L. Jackson, in *Cambridge Biblical Essays,* 1909, p. 454) is not as "chaotic" as it once was. There is more general agreement than ever on the "two-sources hypothesis" or the "two-document theory," which holds that Mark's Gospel and a collection of *logia* or "sayings" called Q (*Quelle*, "source") lie behind Matthew and Luke. Sanday begins his discussion with the words: "We assume what is commonly known as the 'Two-Document Hypothesis'" (*Oxford Studies*, p. 2).[2] It must not be assumed, however, that the two-document theory rules out all use of the oral tradition which was once (*e.g.*, by Westcott, and still held by A. Wright, *Gospel According to St. Luke in Greek*) considered sufficient to explain the whole problem. "Justice must, however, be done to a theory which at one time seemed to promise a full solution of the synoptic problem" (Holdsworth, *Gospel Origins*, p. 17). The effort of modern synoptic study is to get back to the sources of our knowledge as far as possible, to the "sources of sources," if we can (cf. Patton, *Sources of the Synoptic Gospels*, 1915). The gospels did not create Christ or Christianity any more than Paul did. This much we have learned from the "Jesus or Christ" controversy (cf. *Hibbert Journal Supplement* for January, 1909). The gospels reveal the struggle

[2] The data for this theory are given with great detail and clearness by Hawkins, *Horæ Synopticæ, or Contributions to the Study of the Synoptic Problem*, 2d ed., 1909; Sanday and others, *Oxford Studies in the Synoptic Problem*, 1911; Holdsworth, *Gospel Origins: A Study in the Synoptic Problem*, 1913; Moffatt, *Introduction to the Literature of the New Testament*, 1911; Burkitt, *Gospel and Its Transmission*, 2d. ed., 1907; Stanton, *The Gospels as Historical Documents*, Part II, 1909.

to apprehend Jesus as the revelation of the Father going on in the minds of the disciples themselves while Jesus was with them. "It has been aptly said that at the beginning of Christianity there stand neither book nor letter, but spirit and personality" (H. L. Jackson, *Cambridge Biblical Essays,* p. 423). "Jesus himself had not left a line behind him, and as for the gospel message it was proclaimed exclusively by word of mouth." These books, when they were written, were designed "to hold fast that which had been delivered to them —the words of Jesus and the events of his life" (Von Soden, *The History of Early Christian Literature,* 1906, p. 121).

No books ever written mean so much to modern men as the Synoptic Gospels, for, if they go, John's Gospel goes. We can find room for John's picture of Christ only on the basis of the synoptic tradition, and John's Gospel, in my opinion, is the greatest book in all the world.

III. The Priority of Mark: It is not claimed that Mark's Gospel possesses the literary charm of Luke's Gospel, which Renan considered the most beautiful book in the world (cf. Hayes, *The Most Beautiful Book Ever Written,* 1913). We may agree with Von Soden about Matthew's Gospel that "it became the chief gospel, the work which took the lead in guiding this development, and in so far no book ever written is of greater historical importance" (*History of Early Christian Literature,* p. 199). We may admit with Maurice Jones that "the superiority of St. Matthew and St. Luke to St. Mark is that of a portrait by Rembrandt to a mechanical snapshot" (*The New Testament in the Twentieth Century,* 1914, pp. 225 f.). But even so we insist that the Second Gospel is of prime importance for modern historical study. The words of Jesus are true of Mark's Gospel in a special sense that the "first shall be last and the last first." Certainly Pfleiderer will not be considered an apologist for the gospels when he says:

> "It may be accepted to-day, as a certain result of the industrious gospel research of the last century, that Mark is the oldest of the canonical gospels and is the groundwork for Luke and Matthew" (*Christian Origins,* 1906, p. 217).

It is this almost universally accepted conclusion that gives strategic value to the gospel according to Mark. "This is a fact of such great moment that it gives to the gospel of Mark a unique value" (Gilbert, *Jesus,* p. 11). And yet not quite all modern critics agree to the first place for Mark. The chief opponent is Zahn, who holds that the Aramaic Matthew comes first. Zahn argues from Irenæus and Clement of Alexandria that the order of the gospels is the Hebrew (Aramaic) Matthew, Mark, Luke, John (Zahn, *Introduction to the New Testament,* 1909, Vol. II, pp. 394 f.). Augustine had spoken of Mark as "the follower and abbreviator of Matthew" (*De Cons. Evang.,* i:4). Griesbach, Baur, Hilgenfeld, and Holsten held that Mark followed Matthew. "Holsten's chief arguments for the priority of St. Matthew are of a kind that would appeal to few, if any, minds now" (Stanton, *The Gospels as Historical Documents*, Part II, p. 33). Stanton conclusively answers the present contention of Zahn, whose "position is not accepted by the great majority of scholars" (Holdsworth, *Gospel Origins*, p. 107). Questions of this nature are not settled by a majority vote of scholars, but the chronological order in Mark, as opposed to the topical arrangement in Matthew, argues strongly for the priority of Mark. Besides, the life-like touches in Mark are difficult to understand if Matthew precedes Mark. And then practically all of Mark is in the work of Matthew, who employs another source (Q) for the discourses common also to Luke. The case seems made out. Swete puts the matter succinctly when he says:

> "It appears from this table that out of 106 sections of the genuine St. Mark there are but four (excluding the head-line) which are wholly absent from both St. Matthew and St. Luke; and of the remaining 101, 93 are to be found in St. Matthew and 81 in St. Luke" (*Commentary on Mark*, p. lxii).

The proof for the theory that our present Greek Matthew and Luke made use of Mark and Q is given forcibly by Sir John C. Hawkins in his *Horæ Synopticæ* (pp. 161-197) and in his paper,

"Probabilities as to the So-called Double Tradition of St. Matthew and St. Luke" in the *Oxford Studies in the Synoptic Problem* (pp. 96-138). The ancient writers were uncertain as to the order of the gospels and varied greatly among themselves on the subject. This is shown by the fact that each of the symbols (lion, man, ox, eagle) was bestowed in turn upon Mark's Gospel. But it is interesting to note that scholars of all schools of criticism at the present hold to the priority of Mark. It is probable, almost certain, that Luke includes Mark in his list of authorities to which he refers in 1:1-4. Here Luke speaks as a historian and not as a theologian, and gives us the first piece of synoptic criticism that we have. We are willing to go with Pfleiderer in saying that Luke "took great liberties in the use and arrangement of his material" (*Christian Origins,* p. 223), as he had the right to do, and used great artistic skill in creating the artistic form of the story in noble picture-language, provided we do not imply that Luke discredited his sources.

"The fact that it was possible to work those two chief sources together into one consistent whole is a fresh proof of the trustworthiness of these original documents in all essential points" (Von Soden, *History of Early Christian Literature,* p. 166).

IV. Mark's Use of Peter's Preaching: It is hardly necessary to prove that Mark is the author of the Second Gospel, when such a free-lance as Pfleiderer says bluntly: "Nothing can be urged against the Church tradition that their gospel was written by John Mark" (*Christian Origins*, p. 222). And yet there are discordant voices against this view now "almost universally accepted" (Williams, *Oxford Studies*, p. 389). The gospel itself makes no claim as to the author and he can be anybody, "be he who he may" (J. Weiss). Papias expressly says, on the authority of the "Elder" (Apostle John, according to Zahn, Presbyter John at any rate), that "Mark, having become the interpreter of Peter, wrote accurately what he remembered of the things said or done by Christ, but not in order." Papias adds that Mark was not himself a personal follower of Jesus, but of Peter, and that he wrote down what he remembered of Peter's teaching about Jesus. This account of the origin of Mark's Gospel is supported by statements from Irenæus, Clement of Alexandria, Tertullian, Origen, Eusebius, Epiphanius, Jerome, each with more or less detail about occasion and place. Some locate Mark in Alexandria, most in Rome, when he wrote the Gospel. Irenæus states that Mark wrote after the death of Paul and Peter, but Jerome says that it was during Peter's lifetime and that Peter approved and commended the work of Mark. We know that Mark was with Peter in Rome (Babylon) from 1 Peter 5:13. Peter calls Mark his "son." The Gospel itself shows that much of it comes from an eye-witness. The vivid details and frequent touches about the looks and gestures of Jesus come from one who saw and heard Jesus. Mark's Gospel is the briefest of all; and yet, because of these lifelike pictures, his account is fuller in most of the incidents which he narrates than the other gospels. There is no real objection to the acceptance of the view of Papias that Peter is the source for most of the Gospel of Mark. Eusebius even says: "Mark, indeed, writes this, but it is Peter who so testifies about himself, for all that is in Mark are memoirs of Peter" (*Demonstratio Evangelica,* III. 5). This is probably an overstatement of the case, for there are doubtless other sources used by Mark besides the notes that he had made of Peter's preaching. But in a true sense Mark's Gospel can be called "The Reminiscences of St. Peter Written by St. Mark" (Von Soden, *History of Early Christian Literature,* p. 142). It has often been noted that Peter's sermon, outlined in Acts 10:37-41, is a good summary of Mark's Gospel, which, like this discourse, begins with the ministry of John the Baptist and discusses chiefly the work in Galilee and Christ's death and resurrection. Zahn makes a good deal of the fact that in Papias we have the first criticism of Mark's use of the Petrine material by John the Apostle (Presbyter), the author of the Fourth Gospel (*Introduction to the New Testament,* p. 442). He thinks that John approves what Mark obtained from Peter, but "John hints that when this source of memory failed him, Mark's presentation actually shows want of accuracy'' (*ibid.*). I think that this is reading into Papias's language more than is there. The ''in order'' may simply mean ''incomplete,'' and certainly that is true of Mark's Gospel as compared with Matthew and Luke. If Papias does give us an estimate of Mark's work (and Peter's), we have also one from Luke (1:1-4), as we have already observed. Gospel criticism existed, and naturally so, in the very earliest Christian circles.

V. Mark and Q: If we admit that Peter's discourses form the main source of Mark's Gospel, and that his Gospel is the oldest of the Synoptics, what relation does it sustain to Q (the Logia of Jesus), the other main source of Matthew and Luke? ''Even our preliminary survey of the contents is enough to prove that this gospel is (or was) very much more than a mere editing of Peter's discourses'' (Bacon, *Beginnings of Gospel Story,* p. xx). It is now generally admitted that Q was used by our Greek Matthew and by Luke, though the precise contents of Q are not agreed upon. Some would make it the Aramaic (Hebrew) Matthew of Papias. Others would make it only what is contained in both Matthew and Luke. Others would make it wider still and include part of what occurs in either Matthew or Luke. Streeter (*Oxford Studies,* pp. 185-202) discusses ably ''The Original Extent of Q.'' But what about Mark's use of Q? Q is generally placed before Mark—twenty years before, Streeter says (*Oxford Studies*, p. 219). Ramsay (*Expositor*, May, 1907) suggests that Q was written down during the ministry of Jesus, probably by Matthew the publican. Salmon holds the same view (*The Human Element in the Gospels*, p. 274). Wellhausen considered it "extraordinary" that so little had been done about the relation between Mark and Q: "The problem of the literary relationship between Q and St. Mark must at least be propounded and needs thorough investigation" (*Einleitung in die drei ersten Evangelien*, p. 73). Streeter, after an extended discussion of "St. Mark's Knowledge and Use of Q," concludes that there are "only a few reminiscences of Q" to be found in Mark (*Oxford Studies*, p. 183). One he finds in Mark 1:7 f. (cf. Matt. 3:11; Luke 3:16). Certainly there is no objection to the use of Q by Mark. Since Q was earlier in date, this is quite probably true. Luke made use of various sources (written and oral) for his gospel. Mark did not possess Luke's literary gift, but he surely was only too glad to use all the data that fell within the compass of his plan.

VI. Other Sources for Mark's Gospel:

"Is the second gospel, as we have it, a literary unity, coming almost immediately from the lips of St. Peter, the spokesman of the apostolic band, and consequently possessing first-hand authority in all its parts? Or is it a composite work with a long and complicated literary history behind it?" (Williams, *The Origin of St. Mark,* in *Oxford Studies,* p. 389).

Probably neither of these questions hits the truth. We have seen that Mark did not obtain all his information from Peter, though most of it came from that source. But what about the theory of several "Marks"? Wendling in his *Urmarcus* (1905) and his *Die Entstehung des Marcus-Evangeliums* (1908) advocates the theory of M^1, M^2, M^3 (our Gospel). Williams considers Wendling's theory ingenious and plausible, but too intricate and artificial. "A great deal, if not all, of Wendling's elaborate structure will have to be dismantled" (*Oxford Studies,* p. 403). But it is possible that Mark may have had a "Little Apocalypse" document of early date on a par with Q which he has incorporated in chapter 13 (cf. Streeter, *Oxford Studies,* pp. 179-183). Holdsworth suggests that Mark himself prepared three separate editions of his Gospel, one a rough draft of Peter's discourse at Cæsarea (cf. Acts 10: 37-43), another in Alexandria, and the third (our Gospel) in Rome. This also is ingenious, but not convincing. It must be admitted, however, that the variations in the close of Mark's Gospel lend some color to some of these theories. It is held by some scholars that there is even evidence of the use of Matthew by a later edition of Mark. Swete is willing to allow editorial revision by Mark at some points.

VII. The Original Language of Mark: It was almost certainly the current Greek in which we now have it. Some scholars have suggested Latin, since Mark seems to have written in Rome, and since he uses a number of Latin words in his Gospel. But Greek was used in Rome as elsewhere. Paul wrote his Epistle to Rome in Greek and Marcus Aurelius wrote his mediations in Greek (cf. Robertson, *Grammar of the Greek New Testament in the Light of Research*, p. 54). Prof. J. T. Marshall, Wellhausen, and others have advocated Aramaic as the original language of Mark's gospel, since Mark was a Jew and since he transliterates a number of Aramaic words in his Gospel like *Corban* (7:11), *Ephphatha* (7:34). But Mark both transliterates and translates. A translation would hardly do both (Swete). Mark himself was bilingual and at home in both Aramaic and Greek. Thus he was able to be of such good service to Peter as his "interpreter" (Papias). The modern view is that Mark wrote in Greek. This is also in accord with the description in Papias, who says nothing about an Aramaic Mark, though he does mention the Aramaic Matthew.

VIII. The Date of Mark's Gospel: Here the critics do not agree, though most consider it early. Harnack dates Acts before the close of Paul's first Roman imprisonment (*The Date of the Acts and the Synoptic Gospels*, p. 99). This could not be later than A.D. 63. Since Luke's Gospel comes before Acts (1:1 f.), the Gospel was written in Cæsarea (Acts 24 and 25) and not later than A.D. 60. If Luke made use of Mark, we must go back into the fifties for Mark. If Matthew made use of Mark also, and was earlier than Luke, we must go back to "about A.D. 50" for Mark (Nolloth, *The Rise of the Christian Religion,* 1917, p. 20).

IX. A Triumph in Critical Research: No one would be rash enough to claim that "the literary evolution of the gospels" (Streeter, *Oxford Studies,* pp. 210-227) is now clearly made out at every step. But it is not too much to say that the broad outline is reasonably plain. Harnack, indeed, lamented—

> "The wretched plight in which the criticism of the gospels finds itself in these days, and indeed has always found itself—with the exception of the work of a few critics, and apart from the Marcan problem, which has been treated with scientific thoroughness" (*Sayings of Jesus,* tr. 1908, p. xiii).

Victor of Antioch in the fifth or sixth century wrote a commentary on Mark and said that he knew of no other on this Gospel. It was neglected at first because it was only the work of a disciple of an apostle, while Matthew and John were written by apostles, and Luke was longer and of great charm. But Mark's Gospel has at last come to its own. The brevity, simplicity, and unstudied character of a disciple's notes add to the historical value of the book. "It is seen, too, to be at the basis of the whole problem of the origin and mutual relations of the canonical gospels" (Salmond, art. "Mark's Gospel," Hasting's *Dictionary of the Bible*). Mark's Gospel, therefore, becomes a solid rock on which to stand in the study of the problems connected with the life of Jesus. Criticism has brushed away the fog of mythical theories and we begin with Q and Mark. Thus we can see more easily how Matthew and Luke were written later. Von Soden (*op. cit.*, p. 153) says of Mark and Matthew: "Never has there been bestowed upon men a work of purer literary art—a work in which the artist is more completely effaced by his subject—than in these two original gospels."

Chapter XI

THE LIFE OF CHRIST IN MARK'S GOSPEL IN THE LIGHT OF THE WORLD WAR

It was my privilege to teach a class of two hundred Y. M. C. A. Secretaries in the Fourth Army School at Blue Ridge, N. C., during the month of May, 1918. They were candidates for war work at home and overseas. They represented many professions. There were college professors, pastors of long experience, theological students, college and university students, lawyers, physicians, merchants, bankers, and one moving picture expert. They had one common interest. They loved Jesus, and they wanted to do their bit to help win the war. The Dean of the School, Dr. W. D. Weatherford, asked me to teach the life of Christ so that the men could face their problems with the help of Christ's outlook upon world conditions. I had taught the life of Christ for thirty years from many angles, but never in this fashion. The task appealed to me, and I undertook it and greatly enjoyed it. If any one thinks that the life of Christ is lacking in virility and is unsuited to one who is up against the real problems of modern life, he is vastly mistaken. It has occurred to me to show how the subject developed from this standpoint. Peace has come, but we are still interested in the war. We studied the Gospel of Mark in eighteen lessons. It required no straining after effect to find the message that was needed for the emergency. We can follow the course of the lessons. The material is so rich that only a sketch can be attempted. The points are emphasized that correspond to present world conditions.

I. The Challenge of the Age (i. 1-39)

John the Baptist and Jesus challenged by their message the religious self-complacency of the times, that concealed moral and spiritual decay. In a curious likeness this world war caught the nations unprepared for grappling with the stern realities of life. It required some time for the Allies, and for the United States in particular, to break away from the cobwebs of tradition and to grasp the hand of God outstretched in the darkness.

1. *The Beginning of the Proclamation of the Gospel* (i. 1).—This is what Mark means, and it is at this point that he begins his narrative, probably following the graphic preaching of Peter. He starts with the shock caused by the first news from the desert as astounding to Jews as the fateful news of the closing days of July, 1914, to the modern world.

2. *The Call of the Baptist to Repentence* (i.

2-8).—It was weird like the cry of the eagle. In the wilderness this lone prophet in strange garb, like Elisha of old, denounced the whole nation as apostates from Jehovah and called them back to repentance and to baptism as if they were proselytes from heathenism. He said that the Messiah was at hand to sift the nation at last. The ecclesiastics were angered at the presumption of the Baptist, but the masses were smitten at heart by the truthfulness of his indictment, and were fascinated by the hope of the Messiah with deliverance, as they believed, from the yoke of Rome. A new era had dawned, one that yearned for righteousness.

3. *The Two Men of Destiny Meet* (i. 9-11).—John and Jesus meet at the Jordan, Forerunner and Messiah, the past and the future. The hour was struck, "der Tag" indeed, the day of days, looked for and longed for by Jewish prophet and sage. The Father gives audible expression of his pleasure in the Son. The Holy Spirit sets his seal upon the formal introduction of Jesus to his Messianic mission. History hinges upon the work of pivotal men. Eliminate Washington from the Revolutionary War and imagine the result. Imagine David Lloyd George, Woodrow Wilson, and Marshal Foch out of the war during 1918. Instead of victory, defeat would have been our portion so far as we can see.

4. *The Attack of the Devil* (i. 12, 13).—It was inevitable. The great reactionary, the champion

of the old order of evil, the victor over the First Adam, was not going to allow the Second Adam, without a struggle, to institute the new order that meant freedom and progress for the human race. But the attack was adroit with abundant camouflage as a peace offensive for a compromise agreement. The wild beasts and the angels add to the tragic wonder of the lonely vigil. The devil is ready to fight every man who champions the cause of righteousness and liberty for men and women. Jesus was no complacent pacifist, but chose battle, well knowing the long conflict ahead with the forces of evil intrenched in State and Church. He saw that both prince and priest would stand in his path if he stood for right against might. But Jesus chose the road that led to Calvary. He would not go to the devil's Canossa.

5. *Christ's Preaching in Galilee* (i. 14-39).—John is in prison, victim of Herod Antipas and Pharisaic jealousy, fateful prophecy of what awaited Jesus. But Christ did not falter. The rather he pressed his message with renewed energy, but in Galilee, to get away from the Jerusalem Pharisees, who were envious and hostile. Here he recalled a group of disciples, and soon set Capernaum ablaze with the freshness and force of his preaching and the wonder of his merciful cures—a combination of army chaplain, preacher in the trenches, medical man, Y. M. C. A. and Red Cross worker. Galilee was soon on fire with the new order of things.

II. At Grips with Ecclesiasticism (i. 30-ii. 28)

1. *Observing Rules for Sanitation in the Healing of the Leper* (i. 40-45).—We see here the tender touch of Christ's hand in sympathy and the stern command (like military rules) that the leper report to the priest for ceremonial certificate of cleansing. The Levitical rules for purification bear a striking resemblance to the modern rules for quarantine and sanitation. The preacher or Y. M. C. A. worker must needs know how to obey implicitly military and civil regulations in such matters.

2. *The Conscientious Objectors* (ii. 1-12).—The very success of Jesus in his tour of Galilee aroused the animosity of the scribes and Pharisees, who were on the alert for points to criticize. When Jesus forgave the sins of the palsied man (his sickness, due to sin as is so often true today, alas), the pietistic Pharisees were resentful at his blasphemous claim of divine power. So far from apologizing to them, Jesus healed the man to prove the truth of his claim. He made good by doing this deed. The objectors are always on hand ready to criticize the plan or the purpose. President Wilson had his share of hypercriticism, but he pressed on with his task of winning the war.

3. *Drafting a Publican* (ii. 13-17).—The patriotic Jews detested the publicans who collected taxes for the Herods and for Rome. The Phari-

sees professed amazement that Jesus should call a publican to his service and actually accept an invitation to a reception in his home attended by a motley crew of publicans and sinners. Race prejudice ran high. Democracy had small sympathy in the minds of these self-righteous exponents of tradition who claimed the exclusive partnership of God, Pharisaic Junkers that they were. But Jesus scouted their pretensions and justified his iconoclasm.

4. *The Revolution* (ii. 18-22).—Hatred makes strange companions. Misguided disciples of John join with the Pharisees in criticizing the followers of Jesus for not observing one of the stated fast days, perhaps at the time of Levi's feast. Red tape tries to throw its bonds upon the work of Jesus. John had a touch of asceticism, but Jesus had the freedom of the fields. He would not brook the dead hand of the old dispensation upon the young life of the new order. He burst the bonds of formalism as many an acorn has sundered the rock by its very life. The parables of the bridegroom, the new patch, the new wine, stick in one's mind forever.

5. *Piety in the Open on the Sabbath* (ii. 23-28).—Jesus had the habit of worship in the synagogue on the Sabbath. The church-going habit is one that all men should have. But he would not allow it that men cannot commune with God in the fields—God's out of doors—on God's day. The breath of the trenches is here, where men come

into touch with the realities and care less for the usual conventions. Many a man found God in the trenches who had failed to see him at church.

III. Organizing for Victory (Chapter III)

It is clear that Jesus must meet the Jerusalem conspirators with organization. The spiritual impulse is not enough to win with, though absolutely essential. In the grapple with autocracy, democracy had to learn the lesson of efficiency. Jesus faced the combination of priestcraft and statecraft as the devil's tools to enslave men. It has often been so that those who should be the servants of the people and the champions of their liberty were the chief oppressors of the masses.

1. Defying the Reactionaries (iii. 1-6).—The Pharisees made their plans to expose Jesus as a Sabbath breaker, and were present to watch his conduct in the synagogue. The man with the withered hand was there. The Pharisees regarded Jesus as a dangerous demagogue, a blasphemous trickster and deceiver, the enemy of all the vested interests and privileged classes. The old order stood at bay. Jesus "looked about on them with anger" and accepted their challenge. He healed the man's hand. In a rage, the Pharisees and Herodians, political rivals and foes, rushed out and into each other's arms in common conspiracy to kill the upstart from Galilee who was overturning all their plans.

2. *Popular Excitement* (iii. 7-12).—But the people had come to realize that Jesus was their champion and friend. They rallied to his standard, to the increased indignation of the stand-patters. The men with demons were hailing Jesus as the Son of God.

3. *Choosing a Band of Teachers for Training* (iii. 13-19).—It was a serious task to pick out twelve men who showed some responsiveness to the new ideas and who had stamina enough to stand the coming storm. The Pharisees had their school, but Jesus passed by all their students and chose, after a night of prayer, men who would be less hampered by the Pharisaic environment. But they must be trained, and by Jesus himself. So the Master began his peripatetic school with this group of men. It was a theological clinic-like service in the cantonments or in the trenches. They must catch Christ's spirit and learn his method, and be hardened to endure the dark days that were to come. Leaders they must learn to be, but first they must learn to follow. The Germans said that the United States simply could not produce enough trained leaders to man a great army. But the impossible happened, as the Germans learned at Chateau-Thierry.

4. *Meeting Vicious Attacks with Vigor* (iii. 20-30).—The rabbis had to admit the fact of Christ's miracles. They sought to undermine his power

with the people by suggesting Satan's coöperation. These pious agents of the devil actually charged that Jesus was in league with the devil. The Master replied with pungency and power by showing their utter degeneracy and unworthiness. They had passed the bounds of decency and of forgiveness.

5. *Misunderstood at Home* (iii. 31-35).—The brothers of Jesus felt the sting of the charge of the rabbis, and were actually ashamed of Jesus. They came to take him home as one beside himself, to put the most charitable construction on his conduct. Even Mary, his mother, for the moment felt bewildered by the turn that affairs had taken and had an aching heart. But Jesus found sympathy in those who followed him.

IV. A New Style of Teaching for the Crisis (iv. 1-34)

1. *The Occasion for It* (iv. 1, 2).—It was a crisis, just as Germany faced a crisis in July, 1914, and brought on the world war, planned for a generation. The Pharisees compelled Jesus to veil his teachings, for the time being, in parables, so that the enlightened might understand the mystery of the Kingdom while the quibblers and the hostile would be rendered powerless to prevent his message. Jesus loved to use clear language, but he would not cast pearls before swine.

He wanted to be understood, and urged people to hearken to his words.

2. *The First Story* (iv. 3-9).—The parable of the sower seems simple enough for all to comprehend. It is not enough to have good seed, good soil; prepared soil is also necessary. Children must be taught patriotism if disloyalty is to disappear. The four classes are always present: the callous or cynical, the emotional, the quitters, the responsive.

3. *Private Exposition for the Preachers* (iv. 10-20).—Curiously enough, the apostles were puzzled by the parable, and Jesus had to explain it to them in private. The dullness of preachers and other leaders is often due to preconceived ideas. That is the inherent difficulty in all teaching. The mind is full of ideas, and construes words in a way not meant by the speaker or writer. It was the prerogative of these men to have insight into the mystery of the Kingdom of God. But they must have experience of God to do that.

4. *The Peril of Listening* (iv. 21-25).—Light brings responsibility. It cannot be shirked. America could not stop her ears to the cry of Belgium, France, Britain, and Serbia. For very shame we had to respond, and for our own safety also. The cry of the children on the "Lusitania" will never be forgotten. Words stick like burrs.

5. *The Law of Growth* (iv. 26-29).—The soil is prepared and the sower sows the good seed.

And then he must watch the miracle of birth and growth, the mystery of God. But the plant will grow till the ear is ripened. God works in silent grandeur through the ages, and the puny plans of men come to naught. The crowns of Czars and Kaisers tumble from their heads when their wearers defy God's love for men.

6. *The Expanding Development of God's Kingdom* (iv. 30-34).—We can learn from the mustard seed. Bismarck, the man of blood and iron, was afraid of the imponderables in war. They win in the long run, as the world war showed.

V. Jesus Lord of Life and Death (iv. 35-v. 43)

This lesson raises big problems: miracles, laws of nature, person and claims of Jesus, demons, personality, life, death. But Jesus is master at every turn. Mark's Gospel, though the earliest, has all the real difficulties that one finds in John's, the latest. Peter faced them all, as Mark reports him.

1. *In a Sinking Ship* (iv. 35-41).—The disciples gave up all as lost and were amazed by the apparent indifference of Jesus concerning their welfare. They were frightened, though they had on board the Master of wind and wave. One's conduct in dire disaster is a good index of character. Instance the "Titanic," the "Lusitania." Cowards at such a time brush aside women and children to save their own miserable lives. Could

the disciples perish with Jesus on board? Can we fail if we do God's will? The Fourth Man walked in the fiery furnace. The Comrade in White ministered in the trenches in France.

2. *A Wild Man of the Hills, the Victim of Passionate Impulses* (v. 1-20).—This terror of the tombs, a man without discipline, burst all restraint and defied all effort at control. He seemed a hopeless proposition for Christ, and was in the grip of a legion of demons, like some of the men called in the draft in our country to be whipped into line for soldiers. Some of them were the victims of rum, of lust, of gambling, of opium. One-fourth of the men called under the first draft law were disqualified by venereal diseases. Germany laughed us to scorn. But our government adopted war-time prohibition, drove back the scarlet women from our camps, brought in the Y. M. C. A., the Knights of Columbus, the Red Cross, the Y. W. C. A., trebled the number of chaplains, added science to religion and training. We sent overseas the cleanest lot of men alive. Jesus cast the demons out and let them enter the swine, who went wild at the inrush of demoniac energy and were drowned in the sea, to the disgust of their owners. The man was saved, clothed, and in his right mind, but the hogs were lost. Hence the owners, caring more for money than for men, begged Jesus to leave their region. He had interfered with property rights, which weighed more with these grafters than human life and welfare.

It is the same story to-day. All who fight liquor, white slavery, child labor, and sweatshops come up against this war-time profiteering spirit. It is humanity in the raw; but Jesus is able to save the hopeless cases. He does it now.

3. *The Individual in the Crowd* (v. 24-34).—The great crowd was pressing Jesus from all sides. But one timid sufferer, with a chronic illness, who had tried all the doctors in turn, including the quacks, and had steadily gone from bad to worse, crept up and touched the hem of Christ's garment. Her faith was rewarded and Jesus felt power go out from him. She felt the cure, and Jesus knew it also. It costs something to cure. What a picture is this of the relief work of the Red Cross canteens, of the ambulance service, of the soup kitchens, or the medical corps at the front.

4. *In the Death Chamber with Jesus* (v. 21-23, 35-43).—We have all been there—on the battle field, in the hospital, in the home—with our own holy dead. How helpless we all feel, but how calm Jesus is in the house of Jairus. "My little daughter has it very bad," Jairus had pleaded. And then he came too late. She was dead. But it is never too late. He took the child by the hand and brought her back to life, back to the father and the mother, glorious prophecy of Christ's triumph over death for us all and of the blessed reunion with our loved ones in Christ. It is good to know that Jesus is with us when

the shadows fall and to be able to say the right word to the dying. It is pitiful to see a preacher perform in oratorical pyrotechnics when talking to soldiers who are facing death.

VI. The Campaign to Win Galilee (vi. 1-29)

1. *Knockers at Home* (vi. 16).—In Nazareth Jesus created great astonishment, for his neighbors who had known him as the carpenter could not understand how he could be so great and famous, least of all the long looked-for Messiah of promise. Native talent is often discounted at home. This is true of preachers and statesmen and all leaders. Many a statesman has been elected to stay at home at the very time that his country needed his services most of all. During the war the home front was the chief point of peril. There were those who knocked at the President, at the army, at the navy, at everything. Contemporaries often fail to see clearly the stature of a great man. Lincoln was a notable victim of this blindness till his work was done.

2. *An Experimental Tour of the Leaders* (vi. 7-13).—Jesus had been teaching the twelve for probably a year and a half. He had made two tours of Galilee already. He now sent these men in pairs to make a thorough campaign of the whole country and to try their gifts and powers in the work. It was teamwork, and it was done in a systematic way. They had had a cycle of

teaching, and now made a cycle of work. Jesus followed them to inspect their work. There was the twofold ministry of teaching and healing. The result was a tremendous upheaval throughout Galilee. Inspiration and instruction found expression in organized application that told at once.

3. *Rousing a Guilty Conscience* (vi. 14-29).—This is always a hard thing to do, as hard as it was to awaken the Kaiser to a realization of his sins in the war. Herod Antipas was a typical man of the world with the callous conscience of his father, Herod the Great. In his palace at Tiberias, aloof from the currents of religious life, he yet heard the reproofs of Jesus and his work and wished to see him. But he was greatly disturbed by the wild rumors that came to him because of the tour of Jesus and his disciples in Galilee. People were all agog over the matter, with all sorts of theories by way of explanation. Herod had his own fears that were shared by others. He had been inveigled, probably by the Pharisees, into arresting John the Baptist because of his plain talk about his marriage to Herodias, both having divorced their spouses for that purpose. In the prison at Machærus, John languished for a year, and at times Herod wished to set him free, but Herodias set herself against John (*ἐνεῖχεν αὐτῷ*–literally, "had it in for him"), and finally accomplished her relentless purpose when John's head was carried to her daughter

Salome on a platter. Many a time Herod had his horrors over that sight, perhaps seeing it at night. Now his superstition got the better of him, and he felt sure Jesus was John come to life to wreak vengeance on him for the murder. Wine and women had turned the head of Herod and had cost the head of John the Baptist. There were those who said that John had no business dabbling in politics anyhow. But it is better to have a head and lose it, than not to have one and keep it.

VII. Rest in Work (vi. 30-56)

It is necessary that overworked men find rest, but it is one of the hardest things to obtain. Blessed is the man who invented sleep—yes, and diversion. Concentration is essential to success, but the tension must be taken off now and then.

1. *Reporting to the Leader* (vi. 30.—The apostles had a great story to tell when they came back. Each group was full of its triumphs. Jesus listened as they told "whatsoever they had done, and whatsoever they had taught." Probably they did not report with military terseness. But Jesus heard them through. It was a new experience for them, and it meant much for the future of the kingdom. It was now clear that the work could go on.

2. *Relaxation after Strain* (vi. 31, 32).—The disciples were keyed up with tense excitement and

did not seem to feel the need of relaxation. But the Master wisely said, "Come ye yourselves apart into a desert place, and rest a while." It is a dangerous time just after a great effort has come to an end. Conservation of energy is absolutely necessary for further work. This is true of the preacher and of the soldier. When the men troop back from the front line trenches after days of fighting they need the most skillful handling. Some are dazed from shell shock, some are bruised and wounded, some are literally worn out. But for the medical corps, the Red Cross, and the Y. M. C. A. workers at the front, many of them would be lost forever.

3. *The Interruption of the Crowd* (vi. 33, 34.—Some leaders are seclusive and hate the common crowd of folks. Lord Kitchener had that reputation. Others, like Lloyd George, are of the people. There are always a lot of silly folks who run after the heroes of the hour. So here the curious crowds ran round the lake and got to the eastern side, near Bethsaida Julias, before Jesus came with the twelve. This spoiled the plans for a quiet outing on the grassy hills. Jesus could still have left the rude mob and have gone on up into the mountain. He was tired, and so were the twelve. But Jesus loved the common people and would not disappoint them. So he taught them.

4. *Meeting an Emergency in a Food Crisis* (vi. 35-44).—By mid-afternoon Jesus had a huge hungry crowd on his hands. He could have sent

them back to Capernaum or to the neighboring villages. But, instead, he took the little handful of loaves and fishes that a boy had brought and multiplied them to feed the multitude. If Mr. Hoover could have done this for Belgium, no children need have starved, and we should not have been compelled to "Hooverize" at home. The impossible was rendered possible by Jesus our Lord, Master of the forces of life. He brought order out of chaos, and the groups in gay colors on the hillside were like flower beds.

5. *Meeting a Political Crisis* (vi. 45, 46).—Crowd psychology is an interesting study. But the mood of a mob is a dangerous storm center. Jesus saw the peril and diverted the popular clamor to make him king instead of Tiberius. Such a political revolution would ruin the spiritual mission of Christ. So Jesus sent the disciples away in a boat to Capernaum and then moved among the multitude to get them to go away also. There was dynamite in the situation. The Master went up alone into the mountain to talk with the Father. No one on earth really understood Jesus at this moment of apparent triumph. Lincoln was a man of prayer as he bore the brunt of the battle of freedom. Wilson, likewise, is known to have sought God's help in the crisis of the war.

6. *Christ to the Rescue* (vi. 47-52).—the disciples were caught in the storm at sea, and at night. It was a dark and dangerous hour. It

was made more weird by the sight of one walking on the water about 3 A.M. and coming toward the boat, a phantom, so it seemed. They cried out in fright. Christ reassured them and quieted the storm and their fears. Soldiers tell of angels at Mons and of a hero of '70 who helped the French at Verdun. But certainly God is at work in his own way to-day in history. We can call on him with confidence.

7. *Back at Their Old Tasks* (vi. 53-56).—The news quickly spread that the Master was back again. New crowds gathered. The sick were to be healed, the sorrowing to be comforted. So we press on in life. So we push on to victory. There is joy in the familiar work in the world.

VIII. Breaking Traditions (Chapter VII)

Precedents are not always to be smashed. The reformer must not be a bull in the china shop. Destruction is not always construction. But sometimes it is. Respect for what is revered may demand wrenching of familiar ties.

1. *Red Tape and Rascality* (vii. 1-23).—The forms of law may be used to cover crime. Religious rites may hide real rottenness of life. A spying committee came up from Jerusalem to investigate the conduct of Jesus. These Pharisees were punctilious on all points of religious etiquette. Their insistence on washing the hands before eating (a fine habit in itself) was not on

grounds of sanitary cleanliness, but as a means of saving the soul. They cared for the tradition of the elders, not for freedom from bacilli of disease. They made ceremonialism more important than spirituality or morality. They were slaves of rules, like a military leader who suffers defeat rather than win in a new way not in the accepted military regulations. Jesus rose in righteous wrath against these pious grafters who used corban as a trick to cheat their own fathers under the pretense of loyalty to God. They were like corporation lawyers who are hired to dodge the law.

2. *Overcoming National Prejudice* (vii. 24-30).—Jesus was in heathen territory outside of Palestine. But he could not escape notice and obtain rest. He rose above the Jewish prejudice against Gentiles and blessed the Syrophenician woman's daughter after a delightful bit of raillery. The Great War has done much to break down walls of prejudice between races and nations.

3. *Private Treatment for Special Cases* (vii. 31-37).—There are no hard cases for Christ. But Jesus took this deaf and dumb man aside privately and treated him in a special way. Personal treatment is essential to religious work. One must study his man as well as his message. The touch of Christ's hand was soothing beyond words. Jesus is in retreat still in Decapolis, away from Galilee, from Herod, from the Pharisees.

IX. Training Leaders (Chapter VIII)

1. *Repetition and Routine* (viii. 1-10).—There is always much of drill and of sameness in disciplinary training. Jesus repeated his miracles and his sayings. He met the demands of each day with no desire for mere novelty. A large part of life is taken up with tasks that recur day by day. Jesus fed the five thousand near Bethsaida Julias, and he fed the four thousand in Decapolis. Matthew and Mark record both. But we must not think that the Master took the repetitions in his work as a matter of course. Preachers, teachers, doctors, trained nurses, Y. M. C. A. and Red Cross workers are all in peril of losing zest in the humdrum routine of their work. Each case and each occasion has its own color and interest.

2. *Captious Criticism* (viii. 11-13).—Criticism is valuable and is inevitable. One cannot help forming opinions about persons and principles, but one can take the trouble to try to be just. Every one who does public work invites criticism and must take his share of it. But the Pharisees attack Jesus as soon as he crosses over to Galilee. They demand the impossible as proof of Christ's claiming a sign from heaven. The government is often asked to do the impossible. Ours came near doing it in putting two million men in France in six months. But Jesus could only sigh in

spirit as he met the chill air of this useless demand.

3. *Discouraging Material for Leaders* (viii. 14-21).—Every teacher has his moments of despair over his pupils. And yet new leaders must be trained. One has to use the material at hand. Men cannot be made to order. But the dullness of the disciples concerning the leaven of the Pharisees, of the Sadducees, and of Herod Antipas, cut Jesus to the heart. It seemed like a hopeless task to go on to higher things. But Jesus did go on, and these men justified his perseverance. Out of failure success is wrung at last.

4. *Seeing by Degrees* (viii. 22-26).—The gradual opening of the blind man's eyes is like seeing the point. Some men catch it slowly. But Christ made him see clearly in the end. He finished the task.

5. *Loyalty Under Test* (viii. 27-30).—Jesus had long before told the disciples of his Messiahship. But they had seen popular favor wane. Jesus was not the Messiah of the Pharisaic type. On the spur of Mount Hermon he pressed the twelve for their opinion of him now. Were they loyal after all that they now knew? It was like testing leaders who had been exposed to pro-German propaganda. Peter's noble speech voiced the seasoned conviction of Christ's band of followers.

6. *Bumptious Advice* (viii. 31-33).—And yet, when Jesus undertook to explain what sort of

a Saviour he really was, a suffering Saviour, Peter dared to rebuke him for spoiling all their hopes and plans. It was unprofessional conduct in Peter, treason to the spirit of Christ, and Peter was called "Satan" in stern rebuke.

7. *Weighing Life and Death* (viii. 34-38).—Every soldier has to do this. He must look death squarely in the face and make terms with this enemy of man. Jesus offers the true philosophy of life, that of sacrificial service, the very thing that Peter had failed to grasp. It mattered little to a man if he gained the world (as the Kaiser tried to do), and lost his soul, his real life. The paradox of winning life is to be willing to lose it for others. We are not justified in saying that the soldier wins eternal life by dying for his country. But it is true that many a man, as he goes over the top, makes the great surrender to God in Christ, that does save his soul.

X. The Glory on the Mountain and the Shadow in the Valley (ix. 1-32)

1. *Conduct in the Crisis* (ix. 1).—The kingdom will come, is coming all the time, will come in final glory some day. It is not clear to what Jesus refers here. He may be thinking of the Holy Spirit at Pentecost, of the destruction of Jerusalem, hardly of the end of the world, since some were still to be living. But the main thing is to be ready for whatever comes.

2. *A Foretaste of Victory in the Face of Defeat* (ix. 2-13).—The transfiguration came at a time when Jesus faced death not more than six months ahead. He was in retreat to bide his time and to train his disciples for his departure. The three, Peter, James, and John, on this occasion were allowed to see the glory of Jesus to steady their faith in the hour of darkness that was coming, so that they could strengthen the rest. They were the inner circle; but they seemed unworthy of their privilege by reason of their slumber and dullness. Jesus held high converse with Moses and Elijah concerning his death, which the disciples had utterly failed to understand. Great problems are often above the grasp of the average man.

3. *Out of the Clouds and Back in the Trenches* (ix. 14-29).—The aëroplane comes down to earth. While the Master was on the mountain, the nine left below failed to cure a stubborn case of epilepsy. They had wrought cures before, but this time forgot to pray. They could not heal the boy in a mechanical fashion. They were puzzled at their own failure, as a general sometimes cannot understand his defeat. Jehovah, the God of battles, must be taken into account. In this case the father had little faith in Jesus at first, because of the failure of the nine.

4. *Telling the Secret Once More* (ix. 30-32). —The disciples must be told of Christ's death,

even though they fail to understand it. The truth must be faced squarely.

XI. Social Disorders (ix. 33-x. 31)

Jesus went on with his program in spite of the lack of sympathy from his disciples.

1. *Selfish Interest before Service* (ix. 33-37).—The disciples were agnostics about Christ's death, because that idea interfered with their theology and their plans of promotion. They were actually disputing about the "jobs," like politicians before the election or generals before victory. Jesus caught them in the very act, much to their shame, and took them to task about it. They had to learn that the greatest was he who served most. It is not the law of the jungle, but the law of love that counts in the scale of real greatness. The child points the way for us all.

2. *Sectarian Narrowness* (ix. 38-50).—The zeal of John (the apostle of love, alas) led him to advance his claim to primacy by showing how he had rebuked a man, who was not in their circle, for casting out demons in Christ's name. He did the work and in Christ's power, but was not one of the twelve. Denominationalism is inevitable in a democracy where free opinion finds expression. It can be overdone, but cannot be prevented. Enforced conformity is far worse than freedom with all its vagaries. But we must all learn the lesson of live and let live. We must learn to

thank God for what others do and to coöperate with all who work for Christ, when we can do so without sacrifice of principle. Jesus rebuked sectarian narrowness sharply.

3. *The Problem of Divorce* (x. 1-12).—Jesus guarded the sanctity of marriage. No modern problem is more acute than this. Modern civilization turns on the integrity of the family. Every upheaval like the world war disturbs the family equilibrium and raises fresh problems like war brides and war babies. But fidelity to the marriage relation is essential to human happiness and progress. The Pharisees tried to entrap Jesus with this problem, but they failed utterly.

4. *The Bother of Children* (x. 13-16).—So the disciples thought. They found the children in the way of Jesus and of their work, as preachers, alas, sometimes feel about children at church. But Jesus was at once indignant that children should be kept away from him. His arms and his heart were always open to them. Woe to those to-day who keep children away from Christ. What shall one say about those who cut off the hands of the children or who hold them up on the point of the bayonet?

5. *The Grip of Money* (x. 17-31).—It was a noble young man who won the love of Jesus at sight. He was clean and strong and winsome. But he worshipped the money devil and did not know it until Jesus revealed his idolatry to him. And then, when the issue was made, he clung to

his money and left Christ. There is no hope for the miser who clutches his bag of gold. Blood money is on the hands of many of those who pass muster in good society, who even sit in our churches, blood money wrung out of the toil of women and little children.

XII. Jealous Leaders (x. 32-52)

1. *Jesus Going to Meet His Destiny* (x. 32-34). —It was more than premonition of what was to come, such as men going into battle may have. Jesus knew beforehand what the rulers were going to do. Jesus could not fall in with the plans of the Pharisees. His kingdom was to be spiritual and universal. So he went on to Jerusalem with a look that caused amazement and fear in his followers. He made a point of revealing his death with the rainbow of promise about his resurrection, but the twelve could not grasp it.

2. *Ambitious Scheming* (xi. 35-45).—It seems incredible that at this time James and John (with their mother) could have requested the two chief places in Christ's kingdom for themselves. They misunderstood Christ's idea of the kingdom and were seeking their own preferment rather than the common good. It is the cry of privilege rather than the spirit of sacrifice and service that Jesus shows in his atoning death that he demands in those who follow him in the baptism of death. James and John blandly accept that to gain their

wish, so bent were they on their ambitious purpose. The ten were indignant at this spirit. Jealousy among leaders has often ruined a great cause.

3. *On the Scrap Heap* (x. 46-52).—The picture of blind Bartimæus, a mere wayside beggar, crying out for help as Jesus passed by, is like that of so many to-day in stricken Europe. They have been ruthlessly brushed aside by war. But Jesus thought no cases unworthy of help. He mended the broken earthenware at every turn, as we must repair humanity in every possible way now.

XIII. The Conquering Christ (xi. 1-25)

1. *Throwing Down the Gauntlet* (xi. 1-11).—The triumphal entry of Jesus into Jerusalem on Sunday morning of Passion Week was planned by the Master to show his power with the people and to make public claim to be the Messiah. He well knew what the outcome would be and wept over the city in this hour of glory. His hour had come, the climax of all, and he would take the consequences. The people from Galilee went wild with joy and the Sanhedrin were terror-stricken.

2. *Unpreparedness* (xi. 12-14).—The barren fig tree is a parable of unreadiness. Jesus blasted it as an object lesson for the disciples and for us.

3. *Attacking Graft and Vested Interests* (xi.

15-19).—The very temple had become the scene of traffic, and the money sharks plied their trade there and made it a den of robbers. The robber barons stop at nothing to coin money, whether man or beast, woman or child, State or Church, shells or aëroplanes, khaki or ships, coal or wheat. But Jesus exercised his authority to cleanse the temple, to the consternation of the guilty grafters, an exhibition of Messianic reform.

4. *Victorious Faith* (xi. 20-25).—Mountains have to be removed, for the grafters and traitors pile them up. Napoleon said, "There shall be no Alps," and went over to Italy. Wilson laughed at the submarines, sent our men over in safety, and the war was won. "This mountain" is always the trouble. We can attack easily and confidently some other mountain at a distance. But we quail at "this mountain" right across our path.

XIV. The Rout of Christ's Enemies (xi. 27-xii. 44)

For the moment Jesus is master of Jerusalem, to the dismay of the Sanhedrin.

1. *The Ecclesiastical Leaders Challenge Christ's Claims* (xi. 27-xii. 12).—The people came early to the temple to get standing room, and hung on the words that fell from his lips. The rulers determined to demand Christ's authority for his teaching and put him on the defensive. He had

no technical authority to teach. But the trap set for Jesus caught themselves when he referred to John the Baptist, who had given Jesus all the human introduction that he had. John's name was still a power with the people. The rulers were caught on the horns of the dilemma and left Jesus master of the situation. Trimmers always get the worst of it.

2. *Pharisaic Students and Herodians Likewise Fail to Ensnare Jesus* (xii. 13-17).—These disciples of the Pharisees were adepts in verbal jugglery. They had learned from the Pharisees. It was unpopular to pay taxes to Cæsar, but high treason to refuse. This trap was set for Christ with great skill. But Jesus recognized the rights of both God and Cæsar, Church and State, to the utter discomfiture of the quibblers.

3. *The Sadducees Bring a Theological Knot to Christ* (xii. 18-27).—They had often troubled the Pharisees with a conundrum about the resurrection. They knew that Jesus taught the resurrection as did the Pharisees. But the Sadducees are held up to ridicule and the resurrection is proved to the joy of the Pharisees.

4. *A Point of Law Raised by a Lawyer* (xii. 28-34).—One Pharisaic lawyer now rallied and offered his services against Jesus. He proposed a legal problem, but had to agree with the answer of Jesus and was left stranded.

5. *Jesus Turns the Tables on His Enemies* (xii. 35-37).—The divinity and humanity of the Mes-

siah are involved in the words of David (Lord and son of David) that Jesus propounds. The multitude enjoyed the defeat of the Sanhedrin.

6. *Exposure of the Hypocrites* (xii. 38-40).—In a matchless indictment (Cf. Matt. xxiii.) Jesus laid bare the hypocrisy of the rabbis, who stopped at nothing to feather their own nests, even devouring widow's houses. With long prayers they preyed on helpless women.

7. *The Loyalty of the Poor* (xii. 41-44).—The picture of the poor widow who gave her all is immortal. In the great war many another widow gave her all for God and country.

XV. The Abomination of Desolation (Chapter XIII)

Jesus was left victor over the Sanhedrin. But he knew that his death was certain.

1. *Pleasantry Turned to Tragedy* (xiii. 1, 2).—The tensity of the strain was relieved, as they passed out of the temple, by words about the beauty of the buildings, as is natural in such a moment. But Jesus foretold the destruction of this wondrous temple, to the amazement of the twelve.

2. *The Time and the Sign of the Tragedy* (xiii. 3, 4).—On the Mount of Olives they could look back on the city and the temple, scene of Christ's recent triumph. Four of the disciples ask Jesus about his dire prophecy of destruction and the

sign of the calamity. Three great catastrophes confront them (Christ's death, destruction of Jerusalem, end of the world), some connection between them.

3. *Apocalyptic Reply of Jesus* (xiii. 5-37).—It was a hard question to answer, and yet Jesus did, but in symbolic language. The Jews had already many apocalyptic writings (Daniel, Ezekiel, parts of Enoch) that dealt with eschatology. This "little Apocalypse" of Jesus follows the general style. But this is not the main element of the teaching of Jesus. Jesus had a world program (verses 9, 10), and it is not proper to say that he expected the sudden collapse of all things right away. The destruction of Jerusalem and the end of the world are blended like a picture and are hard to separate here. We must recognize perspective. The destruction of Jerusalem was to come before that generation was over (verse 30), but the end of the world was not yet, and the precise time uncertain and unknown even to Jesus while on earth (verse 32). Meanwhile we must watch and pray, work and wait, and be ready.

4. *The World War and the Second Coming of Christ.*—Many thought that Jesus was certain to come before peace was made. But there was absolutely no ground for such a belief. Jesus will come in person, but it will be in his own good time. It is not for us to set times and seasons. It is for us to be ready and meanwhile to push

on the work of making earth like heaven. Kaiserism (scientific barbarism) did look like the abomination of desolation, it must be confessed.

XVI. The Betrayer (xiv. 1-52)

Traitors are always on hand. Jesus had Judas, America had Benedict Arnold, France had Bolo, and Russia traitors innumerable. Things seemed topsy-turvy now after Christ's discourse.

1. *Change of Plan by the Plotters* (xiv. 1, 2).—It was like the Prussian Junkers after the first battle of the Marne. They had not counted on this phase of the situation. The popularity and prowess of Jesus made the Sanhedrin decide to put off the attempt to kill him till after the Passover, when the sympathizers and followers of Jesus would be gone.

2. *A Woman's Insight and Tender Ministry* (xiv. 3-9).—The conduct of Mary of Bethany at the feast in honor of Jesus exasperated Judas, who was already out of sorts because Christ would not go on with a political program. It was a rude thing that Judas said about Mary's deed, but the other disciples took his view. Only Jesus took up for Mary and showed that she really understood him about his death. Jesus was grateful for her gracious act and glorified it. The impracticable is often the most practical. Florence Nightingale knew more than the military leaders.

3. *The Sanhedrin's Windfall* (xiv. 10, 11).—

The rôle of the traitor is so contemptible that one marvels that it is ever played. And yet in a crisis some men yield to it. Motives are usually mixed, as in the case of Judas. The Sanhedrin welcomed him while they despised him. The bribe was only the price of a slave. The Sanhedrin looked on Judas as a sort of dispensation of Providence.

4. *Preparing for the Passover* (xiv. 12-16).—In reality Jesus was preparing for his own death, as he fully understood and with utmost dignity.

5. *Pointing Out the Betrayer* (xiv. 17-21).—To the rest it was like a bolt out of the blue. To Judas it was proof that his crime was known, and yet he bluffed the matter out and went on with his plot. It was too late to draw back. In the shock the others failed to observe the pointing out of Judas, who left.

6. *The Blood Bond* (xiv. 22-25).—Jesus in symbolic form gave the disciples the covenant of blood. They all pledged loyalty by the bread and the cup, like the soldier's oath of allegiance (sacramentum).

7. *Desertion Foretold* (xiv. 26-31).—Jesus foresaw it and warned the disciples. Betrayal by one and desertion by the rest were the cup of Jesus from the twelve. Peter's vehement profession of loyalty till death was taken up by all.

8. *Christ's Victory over the Tempter* (xiv. 32-42).—Jesus was clearly to be left alone, and it was the Tempter's time to come again as he

did. A great leader has lonely hours and sleepless vigils. Jesus fought the battle to victory in Gethsemane with no help from his jaded followers. He gave up wholly to the Father's will.

9. *The Surrender* (xiv. 43-52).—It had to be voluntary, if his death for sinners had moral value. He showed his power and then gave himself up, to the dismay of Peter and the rest, who fled in terror.

XVII. The Condemnation (xiv. 53-xv. 20)

1. *The Ecclesiastical Inquisition* (xiv. 53-65).—Others have followed in the Master's steps. Paul later stood before this same Sanhedrin. John Hus, of Prague, defied the Roman hierarchy, and even now his spirit is redivivus in Bohemia, set free at last. Now in Oxford a monument stands where Cranmer, Ridley, and Latimer were burned. Martin Luther defied Pope and King, and his spirit is still mighty among men. The Sanhedrin constituted themselves a court of prosecution and violated all the forms of law to compass the condemnation of Jesus, the model court of inquisition for all time. The Jewish religious leaders caused Christ's death. They had no charge, no proof, no power to kill. But they put Jesus on oath about his claim to be the Son of God and condemned him for that. Perhaps the Sanhedrin were glad to "get even" with Jesus by this vote, and they were loath to forego the

form of condemnation. They gleefully took vengeance on Christ.

2. *Peter's Cowardice* (xiv. 66-72).—It is a mournful story, and Peter's shame caps the treachery of Judas. They were all "deserters," but John and Peter came back. And then Peter, hiding in the crowd like a spy, caught unawares, lied like a trooper and finally cursed Jesus as he had predicted. It was pitiful beyond words, this "yellow streak" in Peter; and Jesus only looked at him in sorrow.

3. *The Civil Trial* (xv. 1-15).—This is what mattered. The "church" trial was spite-work. This meant business; but it was crooked business, as Pilate soon saw. The Sanhedrin and Pilate reveal their worst traits and show their contempt for each other. Pilate is really afraid of his own part, as many another judge has been who gives decisions as the tool of his masters. Under the threat of Cæsar, Pilate surrendered. He knew that Jesus was not a rival of Cæsar and that the Jews knew it. He did not know what sort of a "king" he was, and yet he was afraid not to let the Jews have their way. They could report him to Cæsar for dismissing a man guilty of high treason in opposition to the Emperor. Jesus is the only noble figure in this scene, and he will judge both Sanhedrin and Pilate. Pilate made a mockery of Roman law and justice, and the Sanhedrin eagerly called down Christ's blood on their heads and, alas, upon the people, as many

another ruler has made his people suffer for his own sins and plots and crimes.

4. *Ruthlessness* (xv. 16-20).—Jesus was turned over to the Roman soldiers, who nagged him for sheer deviltry just because they could. They heaped wanton insults upon Jesus to show their own rough power. But the crown of thorns shines through the ages as a crown of glory.

XVIII. Defeat Turned into Victory (xv. 21-xvi. 20)

1. *Christ's Via Dolorosa* (xv. 21-23).—Christ was crucified as a blasphemous imposter and a presumptuous pretender to the crown. As we see it now, Jesus was tempted in all points as we are, but without sin. The Father made the Captain of our Salvation perfect through suffering. He suffered without the gate as the offering was made without the camp. Let us go out with him and take our place by his side in utmost loyalty. We must take Christ with us to the camp and to the store, to the desk and to the farm. Christ bore his own Cross at first, as he urged us all to do. The shame of the Cross was manifest at every turn, and was flung in his teeth by passers-by and even by the robbers at his side. But Jesus is King and Redeemer on the Cross, and saves a soul as he dies.

2. *The Darkness and the Death* (xv. 33-41).—The sudden and terrible darkness brought silence for three hours, and finally the sins of the world

broke the heart of Jesus in the desolation. The words of Christ on the Cross ring out yet with piercing power, but none so sharply as the cry of desolation at the withdrawal of the Father's presence. But Jesus died with sublime courage and with full knowledge of victory over sin and death. He prayed for the soldiers at the foot of the Cross as they gambled over his garment.

3. *The Burial* (xv. 42-47).—It was fitting that two members of the Sanhedrin should give Jesus decent burial. Nicodemus and Joseph laid him away in simple dignity. Where were the disciples?

4. *The Empty Tomb* (xiv. 1-8).—The women found the tomb empty on Sunday morning. The angelic visitors took the message of the Risen Christ to the disciples "and Peter." All mourners to-day look with wistful faith toward the Empty Tomb on Golgotha, now rescued from the Turk. The graves in France and Flanders are not without hope since Jesus died and rose again.

5. *The Resurrection* (xiv. 9-20).—These verses are probably not a part of Mark's Gospel, but they bear witness to what the other Gospels tell of the fact of the Resurrection of Jesus. This is the only real explanation of the revival of Christianity, which is still the hope of the world. When the war began, men asked on all sides if Christianity was not a failure. Now the hand of God is seen in the war's outcome, and the door is

open for Christ as it has not been since he ascended on Olivet. Men all over the earth have turned to Christ as their only hope. "Sir, we would see Jesus."

Chapter XII

THE CRY FOR CHRIST TO-DAY

The cry of the stricken world is that of Blind Bartimæus, "Jesus, thou son of David, have mercy on me!" It is clear, general, and insistent. The only exception is the Bolsheviki, who have officially "abolished" God and Christ, because they identify religion with the Russian hierarchy. Since the war has swept on to victory, materialism no longer makes loud claims as the sole interpreter of life. For one thing the millions who mourn for their dead who lie buried in France and Flanders will not believe that death ends all. For another thing crass materialism is now identified with German philosophy. German names like Haeckel and Nietzsche are no longer names to conjure with in the presence of the great world-struggle for spiritual life and freedom.

The reactions of men to the world-war are various and changing. When the cataclysm first swept over the world, men said, not only that Christianity was a failure, but that Christ was a myth and God a monster for allowing such a catastrophe. German teachers, scientists, and theologians, openly justified the Pan-German propaganda for world conquest on the grounds of might, the law of the jungle. The nation that had become the school-teacher of the world suddenly relapsed into the barbarism of Goth and Vandal and Hun with all the refinements of cruelty that modern science could add to the methods of earlier barbarians. Whatever was true of other nations, it was at once clear that Germany was not Christian at heart, but still worshiped at the shrine of Woden and Thor, and that the "good German God" with whom the Kaiser claimed partnership was not the God and Father of all men revealed to the world in Christ and expounded by Paul.

Some were able to see at the start that the issue of the war was far more religious than political, that it was Christ or Kaiser. *Kultur* at the point of the bayonet was the old demand of Cæsar to Polycarp. When offered life if he would say "Lord Cæsar," he persistently reaffirmed "Lord Jesus." Paganism to-day is brutal as of old and changes its form but not its spirit. Christ came to set men free, and Cæsar forever fetters the human spirit. Jesus sets men free by the truth. The Kaiser tried to enslave men by his mailed fist. So the issue was joined and the Kaiser was the new Napoleon. Once more it was Corsica or Galilee.

The German warlords had no doubt of the outcome. They had calculated the steps to a nicety and had left nothing out of account. They even claimed a mortgage on God. They had left nothing out save Christ and the spiritual values which they despised as of no military worth. Bismarck, the man of blood and iron, could have taught the Kaiser better, for he feared "the imponderables" most of all in war and in peace. But Bismarck was now a dethroned idol in the Kaiser's house.

Ruthlessness took the place of righteousness. Treaties were scraps of paper. Mercy was for weaklings. German historians could be trusted to throw a gloss over the necessity of atrocities for a swift victory which would silence all neutral opinion. God was on the side of the heaviest battalions, which were indisputably German. So the juggernaut rolled on over women and children and old men. Little Belgium stepped into the path of the monster, and Britain sent her "contemptible little army" to the rescue. The miracle at Mons was believed by many to be the angels of God. But Louvain and the "Lusitania" were soon names that startled the world. Public opinion was defied and America flouted, till a new Sedan suddenly faced the hosts of the Kaiser, who fled for his life, and Germany was in defeat. God had dissolved that one-sided partnership. The old ethical values remained. Nothing after all had been really changed by the war. Right was still right. Truth was still truth. God was still God. Christ was still the White Comrade of the soldiers of freedom. Liberty lived on in the world.

What had the war done for the religious life of

men? It had done much. It had brought men face to face with reality. It had exposed the hollowness of all show and sham in church life and creed. Criticism of the churches on the part of soldiers has been common, as both Professor Harry Emerson Fosdick and Mr. A. Clutton-Brock have shown in their articles in the *Atlantic Monthly*. Some of this criticism has been flippant and shallow. It is easy to attack and less easy to offer a substitute. The Y. M. C. A. has come in for its share of complaint, and our own government is under fire in some quarters. But it must be admitted that some of the objections made against official and institutional Christianity are well taken. Organized Christianity takes on different forms in different ages and different lands and different climates of opinion. Each one claims to be the best brand of the gospel, and men are prone to judge the original stock by the special offshoot which they know. Hence Mr. Clutton-Brock passes in review the various forms of British Christianity and rejects them all, though he believes in Christ.

It is the old story. The Greeks come to Jerusalem and hear of Jesus. They come to Philip with the courteous request: "Sir, we would see Jesus." Philip was one of the chosen group of disciples gathered by Jesus to be his interpreters to men. Instead of introducing the Greeks (men of culture of the time) to the Master, Philip (Greek name though he had), in a quandary by reason of his Jewish theology and prejudices, went off to consult Andrew as a man of wisdom and counsel. The middle wall of partition between Jew and Greek was to be broken down not by Philip but only by the blood of Christ on the Cross. In a puzzle the two disciples bring their theological problem, but not the Greeks, to Jesus. The heart of Christ is torn asunder by the narrowness of his disciples and the stupendous task of drawing all men to himself, possible only by the magnet of the Cross. Jesus hungered for the Greeks, but he looked through the ages of racial and national hatred and saw that he must, like the grain of wheat, lay down his life that by his death he might make it possible to bury class prejudice, sex prejudice, race prejudice.

Jesus was surrounded by followers who did not know how to bring men to him. It was no wonder. Official Judaism was hostile to him, to his claims, and to his teachings. The proud Pharisee had made peace with Cæsar and sat in the seat of authority and did not wish a kingdom of moral and spiritual values. The orthodox Pharisee, rabbi and scribe as well, held the keys of knowledge and had all the rules of piety laid down for observance by the righteous, while with hypocritical subtlety he evaded all inconvenient restrictions himself unless he could obtain credit in popular opinion for observing them. Jesus stood forth in an age of perfunctory piety and official religion and struck the note of reality and righteousness. He scouted mere national religion, the prerogative of Abrahamic descent, and thus enraged the officials of the state church, who plotted his death. Jesus recognized the rights of the state, but denied that church or state could throttle a man's conscience. He proclaimed the fatherhood of God as including men of all races. The Kingdom of God was thus spiritual and catholic, and it was to be lived here on earth. It was to be applied to all the relations of life, individual, social, political, racial. Jesus was the iconoclast of all time. He smashed autocracy, religious and political, and asserted the worth of the individual man. The soul of man is competent to deal alone with God, apart from Church or priest.

It is needless to say that the teaching of Jesus has not been popular when it has been really understood. The crowds in Galilee left Jesus in a body when they saw that, instead of loaves and fishes, he offered the spiritual appropriation of himself and the incarnation of his teachings in their lives. That has always been the case and it is true to-day. Spiritual Christianity has always flourished under persecution. The marriage of church and state has brought disaster to both and the divorce has had its scandals. It is hopeless to look to any form of national Christianity in the present world-crisis. France has only recently shaken off the load of Romanism. Italy struggles to be free. The United States alone has actual religious liberty for all, where no creed labors under any kind of disability. Great Britain has religious toleration, not religious liberty. Mr. Clutton-Brock scouts the Nonconformists as belonging only to the middle class, usually supposed to be the conscience and the backbone of the nation. Certainly some of these Christians do reproduce the spirit of Christ. Even in England the Nonconformists, whom Mr. Clutton-Brock dismisses with a short paragraph, represent fully half of the Christian forces of the land. In this country, where all religious sects are on a par, these very denominations—Baptists, Congregationalists, Disciples, Methodists, Presbyterians—dominate American life. It can hardly be denied that some of these evangelical denominations approximate apostolic Christianity in many essential points. It must be admitted, however, that they have all fallen short in their social programs and have been more or less timid before political and financial leaders. But the Church of England and American Episcopalians have produced some of the noblest Christians of the ages.

And yet, in spite of modern caricatures of Christianity, which are all too common, the men of light and leading to-day insist that the only hope of the world is an actual trial of the message of Jesus. The League of Nations is one expression of this sentiment and of this hope. The Golden Rule has been kept out of business and out of politics. Diplomacy has been real double-dealing, in harmony with the etymology of the word. But the League of Nations can be made permanent and operative only by the spirit of Christ. The shadow of Bolshevism stalks behind the vanishing ghost of Pan-Germanism. The world has literally been dangled between autocracy and anarchy. The victorious outcome of the war with the Treaty of Peace has for the present removed the nightmare of Pan-Germanism. But it is acknowledged on all sides that Bolshevism cannot be handled by treaties or armies. The only panacea for the maddened masses is the Peace of Christ. They must learn that a new spirit is at work among men, the spirit of brotherhood, of justice, of consideration, of love. The greatest statesmen and soldiers of the age are saying that Christ is now the only hope of the race. Once more the Greeks come and say, "Sir, we would see Jesus."

And Jesus can be seen. He is not invisible to those who have eyes to see, ears to hear, and hearts to understand. The trouble to-day is precisely what it was in the day of Philip and Andrew. There were clamoring voices then that dinned into men's ears their patent cure-alls. Pharisee, Sadducee, Essene, Zealot, Herodian, Eschatologist, Stoic, Epicurean, Platonist (and soon neo-Platonist), Jewish-Alexandrian philosopher, the priest of the old Greek and Roman gods and goddesses, Mithraist, Gnostic, worshiper of Isis and Cybele, adherent of the Emperor-cult, skeptic, atheist—these all wrangled in the marketplace of the world. The first thing to do is to clear one's glasses and to open one's eyes. It was hard then to see Jesus as he was because of one's environment and heredity. So to-day men look at Christ from the standpoint of Romanist, Anglican, denominationalist, sacramentarian, ecclesiastic, theosophist, skeptic, man of the world. Each one sees what he sees or thinks that he sees, and is prone to assert that he sees all there is to see. Christ is universal in his nature, Jew though he was. He belongs to all time and to all men. But one may catch only a partial glimpse of Christ.

If we could brush aside all official and institutional types of Christianity and come to Mark's Gospel and the Logia of Jesus (those parts of Matthew and Mark that are alike), we should start with the simplest form of Christianity preserved in the New Testament. We should still have all the essential dogmas of the gospel. A message without dogma has no backbone and no power. It can be shown that the structure in the New Testament built on this foundation by Peter, Paul, and John, is in harmony with the spirit of it. But let that pass. The point to emphasize here is that no people as a whole has ever seriously tried to live by the principles of the Kingdom of God as taught by Christ in the earliest reports of his teaching. And yet Jesus sternly insisted that men must be judged by the standard that he set up before them. The world as a whole has come to praise theoretical Christianity, but passes by on the other side if a point in detail comes up. The call to-day is for the gospel of action, not of mere words.

The cry for Christ to-day is for something new under the sun. It is for an honest and general effort for men to put to the test the moral teachings of Jesus in the home, in business, in the school, in the state, in international life, yes, and in the church. The thing can be done. The teaching is all there, plain as a pikestaff. It requires only clear eyes to see and honest hearts to undertake the task. If it is done, race prejudice will die, religion will be free from state control, the churches will be democratic in form, they will accept Jesus as Lord and Teacher, class injustice will disappear, capitalist and laborer will clasp hands as co-workers for the common welfare, religious profession will square with actual life, no priest will terrorize the spirit of man, every man will claim direct access to God through Christ, no one will hold back from the cause of Christ what Christ needs of service or of money, loyalty to country will be a corollary of loyalty to Christ, the welfare of the whole world will enlist the sympathies of all. All of this, and more like it, is in the earliest reports of the teaching of Christ. The world still waits for the actual experiment on a wide scale of putting these teachings to the test of practice.

We cannot wait for the wholesale adoption of the program of Jesus for the race. We must each face the whole truth for himself. There is no other way. "If ye know these things, happy are ye if ye do them." Religion cannot be written in a law or carried by a popular election. The goal of the Kingdom of God is to reproduce on earth in the life of a whole people the life of heaven. But the sower sows the seed and it fares differently according to the soil. So it is to-day. Let us not despair by reason of the multiplication of denominations and the deficiencies of organized Christianity. The spirit of democracy expresses itself with freedom and variety. It cannot be otherwise. No artificial union will come to anything. The only justification for the existence of any church is that it is bringing in the Kingdom of God, bringing it to pass here and now in the lives of men and women who are to regenerate the world. Any church that is a mere asylum from the world with no mission to the world will die and deserves to die. It is still true that the only way to save one's life is to give it. That is as true of a church as of an individual.

It is still early morning for Christianity. It is at last time for each of us to try the experiment for himself. The cry is for Christ. He can be found. He stands at the door and knocks. He will come in and sup with every man who pulls the latchstring. He will stay in the heart, in the home, at the plow, in the factory, in the editor's sanctum, in the engineer's cab, in the office of the captain of industry, in the Senate of the United States, in the governor's chair, if the occupant will live by the rule of the road, the narrow way that leads to righteousness here in this workaday world of toil and trouble. Kaiserism has gone. Bolshevism will go if Christ is allowed to come to the cottage of the cottar, the hut of the miner, the palace of the money-lord, the office of the statesman. A little leaven will leaven the whole lump. A few live Christians who are in earnest and unafraid can revolutionize any community and clean up any city. The social program of Christ is the world's hope in the new dawn that has come. But every man must build over against his own house, make his home a heaven for wife and children, and see that his neighbors have the privilege of living in a colony of heaven here on earth.

Chapter XIII

THE ETHICS AND THE ESCHATOLOGY OF JESUS

There are those who are not willing to connect the two words ethics and eschatology in the interpretation of the teaching of Jesus Christ. The publication of Schweitzer's remarkable book, *The Quest of the Historical Jesus* (*A Critical Study of the Progress from Reimarus to Wrede*, translation by Montgomery in 1910) gave a powerful impetus to the emphasis on the eschatological side of Christ's teaching. Schweitzer flatly challenged both the Christ of criticism and the Jesus of history: "The Jesus of Nazareth who came forward publicly as the Messiah, who preached the ethic of the Kingdom of God, who founded the Kingdom of Heaven upon earth, and died to give His work its final consecration, never had any existence" (p. 396). Schweitzer pictures Jesus as a mistaken dreamer who thought that the world would soon come to a cataclysmic close with Himself as Messiah out of the wreck and ruin. He regards Jesus as the child of Jewish apocalypticism without ethical teaching or program save for the brief interval till the consummation (*Interimsethik*). This conception leaves him the most pitiful picture of history instead of the Master of men who has dominated the world. Schweitzer confesses the power of Jesus, but treats Him as still "One unknown" (p. 401) and inexplicable.

The work of Schweitzer made a profound impression upon the late William Sanday, for long the pride of Oxford. He interpreted his views to the British and American public and they have had considerable vogue in some quarters. But Dr. Sanday saw that Schweitzer was wrong in claiming Jesus as all prophet and no teacher and a prophet with a hopeless eschatological bias: "I believe it to be, on the whole, as great a mistake to try to explain everything in the Life of our Lord in terms of eschatology, as it is to treat the eschatology as a mere appendage" (*The Life of Christ in Recent Research,* p. 100). Sanday insisted (p. 98) that it is not only the Sermon on the Mount, but also many of the parables, particularly in the Gospel of Luke, that have a distinct ethical content (like the Good Samaritan, the Pharisee and the Publican, etc.). Sanday also criticized (p. 99) Schweitzer for denying that the current Jewish eschatology expected a political Messiah.

In theology as in other things men swing from one extreme to another. There is an eschatological element in the teaching of Jesus. That is not a discovery of Schweitzer's. What he tried to do was to make it the sole explanation of Jesus. In that effort he has failed. Muirhead

(*The Eschatology of Jesus*, p. 50) holds it "undeniable" that the Synoptists fell into the contradiction of making Jesus say that He did not know the day or the hour and yet that the end would come within that generation. Here Muirhead insists on the inconsistency by maintaining a fixed meaning for the words. He is sure that the Evangelists have confused what Jesus taught in the great eschatological discourse (Matt. 24-25), but he holds that Jesus taught the kingdom as both come and coming (p. 83). Muirhead is positive that Jesus saw "a new and glorious career" for humanity (p. 141). He was no mere professional apocalyptist carried away by fanaticism. His moral passion was beyond our power to grasp and He taught righteousness as the goal of man here on earth.

Dobschütz admits that Jesus "was wrong regarding the outward form of His predictions, and especially the time of God's fulfilment" (*The Eschatology of the Gospels*, translation, p. 185). But was he? That question raises the problem of the use of the apocalyptic method by Jesus at all. One can hardly affirm that He did wrong to employ a method that was so familiar to the men of that time. The very vagueness of the symbolism lends itself naturally to prophecy of the future. But Jesus expressly and repeatedly asserted that the time of the end was not known. He urged readiness on the ground of the uncertainty of the time, not because it was certainly to be soon. And one must not forget that the discussion of the end in the great eschatological discourse blends with that of the destruction of Jerusalem with His own death in the immediate background. It is not always clear which precise topic is in the foreground. Dobschütz appeals to John's Gospel for proof "that his looking out for some external real change is well combined with the finest and best inwardness" (p. 207). At bottom with Jesus the kingdom is within us and comes out from within.

Dewick recognizes the good done by the work of Schweitzer in compelling recognition of the catastrophic element in the teaching of Jesus (*Primitive Christian Eschatology,* p. 216), but he insists on the reality also of the evolutionary conception of gradual development as seen in the parables of the mustard seed, the leaven, and the process of growth seen when we have "first the blade, then the ear, then the full corn in the ear" (Mark 4:26 f.). It is not necessary to be always consistent in the presentation of truth. That is quite too mathematical and mechanical. Jesus was a popular teacher and delighted in paradoxes, even though they puzzled even the disciples. The Jewish eschatology cared little for a life of well-doing while Christ laid chief emphasis upon precisely this point, righteousness here and now as proof of pious profession. "We cannot understand Christ's Doctrine of Last Things apart from His moral teaching nor His moral teaching apart from His Doctrine of the Last Things" (p. 223). That is well said and Dewick adds: "And this could not be said of any contemporary system of eschatology."

Certainly Worsley handles the sources of our knowledge of Jesus with sufficient freedom to satisfy the average modernist. He thinks that "we are far too clever (*The Apocalypse of Jesus,* p. 163) and take ourselves too seriously. The quest for the historical Jesus began before Reimarus and it did not end with Wrede. "It began with the patient workers who pieced together the story of His life, gathered from the very lips of those who saw and heard Him" (p. 165). Worsley thinks that the apocalyptic element has been overstressed and overdone. "The eschatology of Jesus is not to be looked for in His every saying. The picture thus drawn of a mere visionary, who continually looked for, and spoke of events which neither have nor will come to pass, is as far from the historical Jesus as is the Christ of the Apocryphal Gospels" (p. 163). So it is plain that Schweitzer is not having it all his own way. He has himself drawn a caricature of Christ while puncturing much modern criticism.

Jesus urged penitence and faith as necessary in those who sought the kingdom of God. We must never forget that Jesus spoke to the men of his day in Galilee and Judea. He took the language with which they were familiar and charged it with the new message that is to go into the whole earth. "Eschatology has become in the Master's hands but a means to an end, a vehicle for the conveying of ethical and spiritual appeal, an instrument for the freeing of the best in man, for proclaiming the divinely born and divinely directed spirit-life of the faithful and forgiven to be the *summum bonum* for mankind'' (Winstanley, *Jesus and the Future*, p. 396). So then, instead of stumbling at the eschatology of Jesus by putting it to the fore, the truth lies in seeing the apocalyptic as merely the tool by which Jesus forged his teaching concerning the kingdom of God for the life that now is as well as for that which is to be.

There are those who try to save the kernel by giving up the husk. Latimer bluntly says: ''What for Him was a matter of confident expectation has not only turned out otherwise, but, in the shape in which he announced it, is absolutely inconceivable to modern minds'' (*The Eschatology of Jesus*, p. 341). Latimer rejects the personal coming of Jesus a second time (p. 343) and denies any day of judgment. That is going beyond what we know, to say the least. We may be flinging away the kernel with the husk in so doing. The imagery may well be dropped, but to drop the fact also is quite another matter.

But there are others who see nothing of worth in Christ but his ethical and social teachings, who make him a reformer, the Teacher with the noblest ideals yet presented to the world. It is at least interesting to note the two groups of writers, the one on eschatology, the other on ethics, both of whom treat Christ as wholly within their sphere. There is truth in the claims for Jesus as the great Teacher of mankind. The last book by Dr. Wm. Newton Clarke was entitled *The Ideal of Jesus.* He recognizes that after all these centuries of the kingdom of God "we do not find it fully realized in the life of the world" (p. 325), "but we see the ideal of Jesus slowly winning victory after victory." Here we are encouraged to press on. A better day is coming.

President King admits that Jesus does not have an ethical system in the sense of an "ordered discussion of technical theoretical problems" (*The Ethics of Jesus,* p. 275), but he certainly does have an ethical system "in the sense of thoroughly unified and consistent thinking on life, its end, spirit, motives, and means" and he puts all this "with marvelous practical incentive to living" (*ibid*). There are not wanting writers who ignore what Jesus has said concerning ethics because he does not employ the technical terms of the Greek and Roman Stoic philosophers. But such affected superiority betrays a slavery to words that misses the reality. No teacher has touched the great varieties of life with the sense of finality as has Jesus. His teaching is still the goal of the race.

Briggs observes that a large portion of the ethical teaching of Jesus "was given by Him in the form of Hebrew wisdom, in accordance with the method of the rabbis and the wise men of his people" (*The Ethical Teaching of Jesus,* p. 8).

That is true as to the form, but the substance transcends the teaching preserved in the Talmud and the Midrash beyond all comparison. Jesus opens the heart without the use of modern psychological terms because he reads the heart like an open book.

It is true that the ethical teaching of Jesus has a direct bearing on social progress as Dr. C. S. Gardner shows (*The Ethics of Jesus and Social Progress,* p. 18). There are social implications in the kingdom of God. The reign of God is in the heart, but it must find expression in the life. And that reaches other lives. No one of us lives to himself. It is here that much resistance is found to the application of the teaching of Jesus to various social wrongs that are entrenched in custom and even in law. But Jesus must be heard in this sphere also. Morality includes the conduct of the individual towards others as truly as toward God.

Dr. James Stalker insists that "the church" can and ought to "reassert all the plain social principles that underlie all the life and teaching of her Lord" (*The Ethic of Jesus,* p. 393). It is not easy to hold up the ideal of Jesus in the face of those who support the church when the preacher proclaims his message if they are guilty of industrial injustice. The arguments for silence are weighty, but one must have courage as well as wisdom. He should render personal service (p. 395) at any cost and not be satisfied with mere doctrinaire theories of social betterment.

Dr. Stalker insists that while the thoughts of Jesus were colored by the eschatological atmosphere of his time, yet "it was not by apocryphal literature but by the Law and the Prophets that the substance of them was determined; and His whole life, from the temptation in the wilderness to the death on the cross was a polemic against contemporary Jewish thought" (*The Christology of Jesus,* p. 235). That is justly said and is a fine corrective to the one-sided views about this or that phase in the teaching of Jesus.

It is curious how easily we deceive ourselves when we seize upon one or another aspect of Christ's life and work. Those who see in Him only a product of his times ignore that remarkable incident at the end of the narrative about feeding the five thousand when Jesus *compelled* (Mark 6:45) the disciples to depart to the other side, because the people were trying to make him King (John 6:14-15). "The disciples, whose hopes were still in many respects like those of the multitudes, were only too ready to fall in with this revolutionary movement" (Denney, *Jesus and the Gospel,* p 286). After all it is not easy to see all sides of a mountain at once. We must get different angles one at a time. The stature of Christ fills the horizon for us all. No one of us sees all of Him. He reigns in our hearts now and here. He will reign more fully when He comes again. Meanwhile we can hasten His coming by holy living and by pushing on the work of the kingdom of God.

No interpretation of Jesus is true that fails to see the Cross as central in His own mind. He saw what was coming and kept going on toward His hour that was coming. In other words, Jesus knew that he was to be the Redeemer. He came to give his life a ransom for sinners. He was conscious that he was the Son of God and the Son of man. His peculiar relation to the Father is clearly set forth in the Logia, as we have seen. It reappears in Mark, in Matthew, in Luke, in John. The Gospels give the picture of Jesus as the Messiah of the Old Testament prophecy and the Saviour of the world. This claim was early made by Jesus, but was not understood by all. Only by degrees did the disciples come to grasp the spiritual character of the Kingdom and the King. The Acts and the Epistles carry on the growth in apprehension of Christ under the tutelage of the Holy Spirit. The Apocalypse of John shows him reigning in heaven and leading the hosts on earth to victory at last.

THE END